Who is in charge of

YOUR FINANCIAL LIFE

Money principles learned in a lifetime

by

Gordon D. Griffin

Captive Press Publishing

ISBN – 978-1515249726

Publisher's note

This publication is designed to provide accurate and authoritative information in regard to the subject matter covered. It has to be recognized that while principles are involved and seldom change, specifics do change and new laws, methods, financial services and offerings are constantly being presented to the public. It is sold with the understanding that neither the publisher nor the author is engaged in rendering legal, accounting or other professional services. If expert or other advice is required, the services of a competent professional person should be sought.

ACKNOWLEDGEMENTS

It is with gratitude that I acknowledge the considerable help and assistance I had on this book from the following:

My son Lyman, who steadfastly put me back on the right track and kept me focused in my thought patterns so that the book flows a good deal better than it might have. I am grateful for his editing and organizing skills, without which the publication of this book in its present, clarified form would not have been possible.

My wife, Dionis Griffin, who has overseen much of the material as final stages of the book progressed. I have appreciated her editing ability and willingness to help despite the many other calls on her time.

My friend, Val-Rae Christensen, who has been very helpful in her focused approach to my writing during the latter stages of publication.

Thank you, all of you.

Gordon D. Griffin

Table of Contents

PUBLISHER'S NOTE   i

ACKNOWLEDGEMENTS   ii

TABLE OF CONTENTS   iii

INTRODUCTION   v

CHAPTER ONE - Money and Inflation: What You Need to Know   1

    Introduction to inflation   3

    Why inflation is so hard to stop   6

    How inflation can be good   9

    Severe high inflation   13

    Protecting your assets from inflation   16

    The importance of productivity   20

    Taking advantage of inflation   24

    Conclusion   26

    An illustration: The Three Brothers   27

CHAPTER TWO - Money Management: How to Handle Your Money   34

    Expenses   36

    Saving for a rainy day   38

    Income   39

    What to do if you already have debt   47

    More money is not the answer   50

    The importance of not spending more than you earn 52

    What to do if you gain a lot of money quickly   55

    Conclusion   58

CHAPTER THREE - Scams: What They Are and How They Work   60

    The Scammer   62

    Scams   63

    Identifying a scam   66

    Scams perpetuated on a mass scale   74

    Soft scams   80

    Conclusion   87

CHAPTER FOUR - Negotiation: Its Art and Power   90

    The factors influencing negotiation price   90

    Specific ways to negotiate for different items   96

    Negotiating bank foreclosures and contractor fees 108

Auctions and liquidation sales   112
Negotiating overseas   113
Conclusion   115
CHAPTER FIVE - Starting a Business   116
My very first business enterprise   117
Personal principles for running a successful business   120
Operational principles for running a successful business   130
Financial principles for running a successful business   136
Conclusion   146
CHAPTER SIX - Long-term Investing   147
The importance of investing yourself   148
How the market works   149
More on the various markets   150
Mutual funds   152
Dividends   153
Analysts, advisers, and account executives   154
The stock market is the best investment   156
The long-term investment strategy   158
How to buy   162
A diverse portfolio   165
Dollar Averaging   166
Buying on margin   169
Buying into the right company at the right price   171
Selling   176
You can borrow money without selling your stocks   178
How many shares to purchase   179
More on mutual funds   179
CHAPTER SEVEN - Advanced Investing Concepts   183
Four-Dimensional Stock Purchasing   183
More on thinking four dimensionally   189
More on investing wisely in the stock market   192
One last word on Mutual Funds   206
CHAPTER EIGHT – Commodities   210
The maintenance (holding) deposit   211
My foray into commodities   213
Interesting facts about "stop losses"   218
The good use of commodities   222
Conclusion   223
ABOUT THE AUTHOR

INTRODUCTION

As the old saying goes, "A fool and his money are soon parted". On that basis I have been a fool quite often during my lifetime. We've all lost money before. However, if you are reading this it is probably because you wish to be a better money manager – to be better at making decisions where your money is concerned. Well, you have come to the right place—this book will show you the way.

What it all comes down to is having the right knowledge. For example, did you know that there are a significant number of people whose only aim and desire in life is to part you from what you have? When you get money above the norm they descend like sharks to see what they can get. Once having got what they wanted, or "picked your bones clean", they are off to their next victim. When they come into your life they will not appear as sharks- far from it! They will likely appear just the opposite! So why am I mentioning all this? It is because knowledge of these people and how to spot them will save you great heartache in the future and the loss of your hard- earned money. The point is that people who are rich know how to protect and hold on to their money; it is their extra knowledge that allows them to stay rich. Knowledge is the key.

So how can we attain this knowledge? The answer, is it is hard. This is because the way life is and the way we would like it to be are poles apart. We are born into this world with zero knowledge and have to learn our way from the ground up. Knowing the way the world really is, as opposed to what people would like it to be (and often represent it to be), is the search of a lifetime. However, the fact still remains that the secret to a good life is to know the way things are, as opposed to what you would like them to be.

I do not claim to be a financial adviser, analyst nor an expert in all the many fields of investing, though I can say that I have been associated with various types of wealth accumulation during the course of my life. It is my hope that I can impart to you some of the principles and knowledge I've gained from personal experience throughout my 80+ years of life. I have been motivated to write this book in the hopes that it will steer a clear course for those of you who want to get into a better financial position and allow you to avoid the more gross mistakes where financial matters are concerned.

CHAPTER ONE

Money and Inflation: What You Need to Know

Let's talk about money; that is what most people want! Where does it come from? What is it worth? Money matters can seem very complex, and indeed there are finer points to its understanding, particularly concerning such topics as the economy, accounting, and banking. The people within these fields each have their own views, which, if put all together, would make the average person scratch his head in wonder at how it might affect him personally. I am only going to give a broad overview in order to illustrate, generally speaking, how the money system works. My goal is to provide this information in simple layman's terms.

How did the money system begin? The earliest form of money equivalent was bartering. The thinking was, "If you give me what you have and I want, then I will give you what I have and you want, so we will both be satisfied."

As people became more efficient at producing food, they gained more leisure time, thus it grew increasingly common to exchange desired items for scarce materials such as silver or gold, or in the Mediterranean cultures, spices from the East; in the South Sea Islands, beads and rare seashells were used.

There is speculation that the Jews introduced the first paper money by way of promissory notes, providing a way of transferring value from one place to another. One wealthy man would give a tablet or scroll to a messenger or other trusted traveler, on which was written a note to another wealthy man some distance away. The tablet or scroll would ask the man at the destination to pay the goods indicated to the person holding the scroll. The Jewish communities were closely-knit, and so the two men would know each other or of each other. They were representatives of the Jewish fraternity and were like bankers with a system of credits and debits. The transferring of goods went both ways, and there likely were fees charged to the one using the note, depending on the amount of goods to be transferred and length of time the note was valid. Through this system, goods could be passed from one place to another without having to actually carry the goods (or the cash) themselves. The notes became the equivalent of today's paper money.

Though there have often been calls for a society that is less oriented to money, there seems no doubt that the modern-day free market system could not survive without it. Countries and closed communities can only survive in a progressive manner with the use of money as a means to smooth the workings of their society and of external trade.

So where does the value of money come from? It is important to recognize that the actual paper and metal we handle in our day-to-day transactions are worth nothing in themselves.

What is it that gives value to money? If the physical money that we hold in our pocket, wallet, or bank account were to be followed back to its origins, we would find that there is some level of work behind each coin and every piece of paper. The value of money reflects work done physically or mentally—by someone. The truth is that all we presently possess derives from work. Money is the grease that enables us to trade and exchange the benefits of our work and efforts for the work and efforts of others.

Money is still like the barter system that originated thousands of years ago. But instead of chickens being bartered for pigs, or physical labor for a meal, we now have money being bartered for every conceivable service or thing. Yet, unless there is work behind it, it really has no value. If it were not so, then we (or a central government) could print all the money we ever needed and we could enjoy ourselves without the need to work or be productive. Clearly, such a system could not sustain itself for long.

You can be certain that, for every product or service we require or enjoy, someone has expended energy, either physically or mentally, to make it available. As individual adults we work and get some payment for it. However, often our work goes to support others who cannot work or are too young or too old to do so—for example, our families, or perhaps the poor, homeless, or unemployed. When we volunteer to help others, we may not want or expect to be paid, yet such donations of time are a form of work and are beneficial to society as a whole. It therefore figures into the final value of money.

The work that we do produces something, even if it is just a vegetable in our garden or a small service of some kind. We may be part of a larger effort such as being an assembly worker, a shopkeeper, an accountant, a municipal or government worker; or perhaps we might entertain others in a way for which they are willing to pay. Work also means effort in thought as well as action. A skilled thinker, such as a money-smart person, can often receive a great deal more money than even an upper-level skilled artisan, let alone the average wage earner. Thinking indeed is a form of work. The number of productive pursuits is almost limitless and embraces all human endeavors. And it is all a type of refined bartering, with money as the grease to makes things go smoothly.

Introduction to inflation

Inflation is one thing about money's value that is extremely important to understand. Inflation is the devaluation of money in circulation. Money can lose value over time, causing goods and services to cost more than they did before. However, it is important to recognize that while the value of money may decrease, the overall worth of things stays the same, meaning that although products and services may cost more (because inflation increases everything, including wages and products), we can still afford to buy it, whatever its price. Except for the influence of increased productivity, the standard of living stays essentially the same. This paradox of inflation is akin to that old saying, "The more things change, the more they stay the same!"

See if you can remember ten, twenty, thirty or even forty years ago. The older you are, the more you will be able see the disparity between the cost of living when you were younger and what it is today. Do you remember what you paid for various products, and services? What did your favorite food cost? How much for a cup of coffee? What did you spend on your first car? Or hotel accommodations? All the normal staples that you use every day, as well as living expenses (such as property taxes and rent) have considerably risen in price.

In my younger days, when I was earning the equivalent of four dollars a week, there was a certain amount of money in circulation in the country. When we compare that to today, the amount of money in circulation has gone up, perhaps more than sixty times in 50 years. The money supply in circulation at the inception of the United States has gone from a few million to several trillion. Such an increase is due, by and large, to the printing of more money. Of course productivity is also higher today than it was then, due to technology and other production advances, which means the overall value of the money has gone up, creating a higher standard of living.

Inflation is often hard to pinpoint, yet we know that it is always there to some degree, and that, as far as anyone can tell, it has always been. The ever increasing upward movement in property values serves to highlight the inexorable march of inflation. For example, the home that I built in 1956 for $7,000 is presently valued, 50 years later, at over $1,200,000!

Another thing to look at is the lowly one-cent piece. It can buy nothing today, yet in early America it would buy a loaf of bread. This means, in effect, that the value of money since those times has decreased by over two hundred times. In the early 1900s it was the norm for a skilled worker to be paid one dollar a day. Yet, as mentioned before, because the prices of other goods were also small, the wages bought essentially the same amount as a higher wage would today.

So how does inflation happen? One cause is a scarcity of labor—in other words, there is a greater demand for labor, but not enough supply. I remember reading many years ago that this happened in the Middle Ages when, at the time of the Black Plague, so many farm workers died that there was not enough labor to plant the crops or bring in the harvest. Land owners could no longer find the help they needed for the wages they were used to paying. Laborers were so scarce that they found they could demand a great deal more for the same work. This sudden increase in the cost of labor sent the prices of all goods up because they now cost more to produce. Because of the increase in prices, the workers were not really better off. That is, although they were being paid more, they were not able to buy more. Very soon, the additional amount of money bought the same amount of goods as before.

Another way inflation can happen is when there is a scarcity of a product. Sometimes the demand for the product increases and supply cannot keep up with the demand. This causes the price to rise, and experience has shown that the prices never permanently go back to what they originally were, even when demand falls off. The prices are pushed to a new, permanently higher level.

The main way inflation happens is when the money printed by the government does not have work behind it. When significantly more money is printed by a government than the amount of work done in that country, it mixes with the money of value, and the worth of all the money is decreased, resulting in reduced purchasing power. For a rough example, if the ideal amount of a government's printed currency in circulation was ten billion, and the government decided to print an additional ten billion in order to pay off some debt, it would cause the value of all the money to be worth half as much, because it was just printed and not collected from taxes (which is payment for the work done by the government) or used in the production of goods and services. The additional money printed, with no basic underlying work behind it, would have the effect of "watering down" the entire currency. The money would now only be able to buy half of what it was able to buy before, because average prices would roughly double. The value of the goods does not change. When this happens, it can be considered a type of stealing by the government of their population's saved money. (How to protect your money from inflation will be covered later.)

The truth is that every country, at one time or another, finds it necessary to print more money. This is OK to a certain extent, as there is always a need to replace damaged or destroyed money, which happens normally in the ordinary course of circulation. Governments also need to make sure that there is not a shortage of actual money in circulation at any given time, because this would cause deflation, unemployment, and lower productivity, as it did in the 1930s. Therefore, printing money has its place. No country can totally eliminate the printing of some currency. And the reality is that on top of these valid reasons, governments also generally allow their paper money to depreciate to some degree in order to have extra money to spend (governments are the only ones who can do this) but it must not be too obvious or done too quickly. Nevertheless, those people who think that their "money wants" can be satisfied by relying on the government to give them money because the government can print as much as it wants are not correct in their thinking, and if this type of thinking were implemented by everyone it would cause disaster. It would cause the government to print too much money without work behind it, which would severely dilute the money already in circulation and, because of the lack of people working to maintain society, and because of the decreased value of savings, it would create a lower standard of living for everyone. I say again, money has no value in itself—only the work and effort behind it. Too much printed money can destroy any society's financial structure.

Why inflation is so hard to stop

One of the reasons inflation in the US, and in all other countries, is so hard to prevent completely (setting aside the fact that the government sometimes purposely allows it) has to do with pervasive human nature. Most people want to be paid more for the work they do than what it is really worth. We are all looking forward to a wage increase, whether or not we have earned the extra pay. And yet if everyone were to be paid more than the work they actually do, the value of all money would decrease, because fundamentally the money is only as good as the work behind it.

Another factor behind the persistence of inflation is that frequently within governments there are programs that require the employment of those who are not productive, but who get paid as if they were. Once hired, these employees are hard to get rid of and naturally have to justify their existence by creating some level of impediment to those that do produce efficiently. It is human nature to justify one's own employment in a given position and avoid being laid off from work. However, such programs can become a burden on the private sector. The first reason for this is that the private sector, due to inefficient government jobs, ends up having to pay higher taxes to support those that impede their progress. Secondly, the private sector is bogged down by requirements to do complex paperwork generated by the inefficient government bureaucracies, making the private sector likewise less efficient. Overall, this lack of efficiency by the government lowers productivity all around and causes higher inflation, which eats away the value of the money everyone gets, including the very people who are employed by the government and are causing the problem.

Whether in the public or private sector, people generally want more: more pay, more goods and services, better working conditions, retirement benefits, medical benefits, and as much security as they can get. Yet they are often unwilling to pay for it by being more productive. Unions, for example, may strike for more benefits—it does not matter if the company cannot afford to pay more. If they succeed in persuading the company to meet the Union's demands, it must either raise its prices to be able to pay the extra money or eventually face going bankrupt. And the rise in prices means that the money paid to the workers will have less value, and thus inflation is created, all because the workers have demanded more than they have produced.

There is no realistic solution to the steady upward movement in inflation. The government tries to grapple with the inflation percentage but it cannot—it is like trying to stop a steamroller with-out a driver. People expect to get more, and everyone feels good about it, not realizing that the real worth of their way of life stays the same. Higher pay is then offset by the higher cost of goods and services so that inflation eventually brings the economy back to equilibrium. Inflation is a great equalizing force. No doubt some un-fairly get more than others, but that is how it has been for the last 6,000 years, at least. Even Marco Polo noted the steady erosion of monetary instruments, such as the promissory notes given out by Kubla Khan in the thirteenth century. Once payments ceased to be made in gold, but were only a promise to pay at some time in the future, the money began to decrease in value.

Ironically, where inflation is concerned, there is essentially very little real fundamental difference between the home that my mother purchased for $500 in 1930 and the $250,000 home that stands there today. They were both purchased at a figure that was comfortable for the buyer. The same is also true for the one-cent loaf of bread two hundred years ago and the two dollar loaf today. Both are acceptable to us at the time of purchase and are relatively the same in comparison to the income and wages we receive. It is really only by being more productive that societies can hope to improve themselves financially in the long run.

In a family home that was built in 1773, and where I often stay when I am in Vermont, there is an old posting hanging up on one of the walls with a list of charges for accommodations and food at an inn (which it used to be). It reads, "Accommodation, four pence. With an evening meal, six pence." We might well laugh at what appears to be ridiculous prices, yet everyone then felt it normal to pay these costs and accept the terms of the boarding houses.

The Federal Reserve has the ability to rein in the US economy somewhat if too much inflation occurs, but they can only do so much. The way they exert their influence is by gradually increasing or decreasing the interest rates of the money lent by the Federal Reserve to the financial institutions of the US. By increasing the interest rates, they make it more expensive for borrowers, which in turn reduces spending, which in turn means less employment, which in turn means that many individuals have to tighten their belts, work harder and spend less. All this will tend to favor conditions that lower inflation. If the decreased spending begins to affect the collection of taxes or stifles business activity, then interest rates are reduced, which in turn allows banks to lend more money for the benefit of those who want to borrow and stimulate the economy. This in turn tends to favor conditions that will increase inflation. However, despite all this, inflation cannot be stopped or directly controlled.

How inflation can be good

Inflation can be a good thing if it is gradual. Mankind does not like recessions—they are painful to too many people. Less profit can be made and governments do not appreciate the lower taxes they can collect. More people are out of work, and because of this there is an even bigger loss of tax revenue. Business and corporations sell less and retrench, reducing the number of employees, thus negatively affecting everyone.

In order to avoid a recession, money needs to be in plentiful supply, allowing for some moderate inflation. The demand for the right amount of money needs to be satisfied, and so printing money is necessary to run a country's financial system. If not enough money is printed, the total machinery of the country's industry and government operation is squeezed and tends to dry up. Governments, as well as corporations and even individual people, create less and spend less when there is less money in the system.

This happened during the first part of the 1930s when many banks had to close their doors and people lost all their hard-earned savings. In the earlier decade, during the 1920s, there was a boom in property as well as in the stock market. Businesses were successful and made profits, and consequently their share prices went up. Speculators sold anything and everything they could, whether it held value or not. Many people thought that their success would go on forever. Money was put into banks for saving and investment. The banks in turn lent the money they had received for new enterprises.

It was possible to gamble on the stock exchanges where the ever-rising prices for stocks were obtainable for just ten percent of the cost of the shares. But then the greed factor kicked in and ordinary people were enticed into making a lot of money by buying new 'hot stocks' which continuously went up. Tremendous paper profits were made, which were then leveraged to buy more stock (leveraging is the use of existing paper profits to borrow more and buy more). Eventually and inevitably the prices reached an unrealistic level, heavy selling took place, wiping out those who were in the market with just a ten percent equity, or ownership, of their portfolio. This created a snowball effect which successively affected all others in the market.

The stocks that had risen the most were those highly speculative stocks, therefore they were the ones that suffered the most. Ironically, the better quality stocks, like Ford Motors and General Motors, had not risen so much and therefore were in less demand. Yet these high quality stocks weathered the downturn and continued paying dividends.

Those who had borrowed money from the banks found it impossible to repay their loans. Those who had put their money into bank accounts wanted to withdraw it to shore up their finances. The banks appealed for calm, but still everyone tried to withdraw their money at once. Soon, the banks' reserve of money dried up and some of them could not even pay their staff. Consequently, they went out of business and those who had any money in them lost everything.

The government of the day decided to let the market take its toll on the previous speculators and, rather than increase the money supply as they should have done, did nothing to alleviate the plight and hardship of the ordinary person who had generally not been involved with speculation.

When there is a recession, governments have to stimulate employment before a turnaround in the economy can take place. How do they do this? They spend money! The government must jumpstart work and effort and the production of goods and services. If they do not, the economy will stagnate and there will not be encouragement for individuals or corporations to push ahead with new ideas and projects. And so the government borrows money or generates extra money by printing it, which, of course, is inflationary. Yet not to do so might create civil unrest, as well as government leaders finding themselves at risk of being kicked out of office. The recession of the 1930s could have been alleviated by increasing the money supply. Some special projects, the most notable one being the Hoover Dam, were paid for by printing more money, which allowed the city of Las

Vegas to escape the impact of the recession, where in fact the boom conditions of the 1920s carried on. Thus we can see that printing money—when it is necessary to increase the money supply and also when there is work to back it—can have beneficial effects on the economy.

Another example of printing money with work behind it happened in Belarus in the 1990s. The average work productivity was very poor because so many people were unemployed and unskilled. The dictator at the time came up with a novel idea: he would employ people to clean up the parks, repair the streets, and start building projects, including a new, state-of-the-art railway station in Minsk, the country's capitol. How did he pay all of the workers? He printed the money! In this way he jumpstarted the economy. Sure it was frowned upon by those economists outside the country, yet the end result was positive in relation to what it would have been had he not done so. People were gaining some skills and the city of Minsk saw significant improvements, which gave the population a sense of pride, particularly when visitors came and noted the great improvements.

Governments need not balance their budget, but they do need to control the money supply. By this I mean that there doesn't need to be income from taxes that is equal to government expenses for the government to function and spend. Rather, they can print the extra money they need, as long as it is in a controlled manner; they can print the difference between the taxes they get in and the amount of money that they need for the running of the government and its programs. This is OK as long as the money is printed in direct proportion to the money circulating in the economy: the working population growth, and the work that needs to be done, such as the construction of highways and bridges, and the funding of the various gov-ernment departments, including the armed forces. Sure it is a bal-anceing act on the part of the government, and although the bottom line is that the money that is printed does have some inflationary effect, still it is expected that there will be some low level inflationary pressure in any event. The printed money is essentially free to the government who can spend it as they like. A balanced budget is therefore almost meaningless except to keep the money supply in reasonable balance. The elected houses will pass some legislation to authorize a certain amount of spending, either for civilian or the military, and instantly it is so. They do not need to wait for the taxes to come in or issue and sell bonds to pay for it because they can just create or print the extra money.

Any printed money does not have to be paid back. How could printed money be paid back? Where would the money be paid, and to whom? Again, once money is created and distributed, it has in effect gone into the melting pot. The money that is paid out usually has only a slight inflationary effect, providing that the amount is not too excessive and that it is going basically to employ people, i.e., there is work behind the money. The amount of money governments hold has been increasing in all of the Western countries of the world as long as anyone can remember, and it is self-evident that it did not all come from taxes or borrowed money.

While the government *can* do this, some might say that the government could also just print money to get rid of the deficit. This, however, would be a recipe for national and international disaster. While the government can and does print extra money gradually, if it is done too much and without thought, it would cause serious problems. The massive amount of money that would have to be printed to pay off the entire deficit would cause out of control inflation. After the inevitable crash (like that which has been seen in some countries in Eastern Europe), incentives for individual, corporate, scientific, and government progress would be severely stifled and the economy would be in ruins. So you see, printing money to pay off the whole of the deficit would be a bad thing, though a little at a time, in a very controlled manner, would be OK.

I estimate inflation in the USA is within the range of 7.2% and 10% compounded annually. This rate is not the official rate as calculated by the government, but the true average, and is largely due to the extra money printed by the government. This rate has been in effect for perhaps the past 90 years, even including the so-called deflationary period of the 30s, and it means that the cost of the average goods and services roughly doubles every ten years. I have come to my estimation of the true inflation rate by a careful comparison of things as they cost in the past to what they cost now (such as the average dollar amount of property taxes charged each year and other costs as will be mentioned).

So why is the official government average for inflation different? One reason is that many inflationary costs are not tracked by government agencies, which only track what it benefits them to track. For example, consider toll fees. If you lived in Boston, Massachusetts, and had to use the Callahan Tunnel daily, the increase in costs over the past 25 years has been equivalent to 7.2% annually compounded inflation. The fees have gone from $0.50 to $3.00. I'm sure you can find similar cost rises over the years in your own experience, whether it be the cost of a cup of coffee ($0.10 in 1957 to $3.50 today), motel charges ($8 in 1968 and between $80 and $140 today), and so many other of your expenses that are not measured by the government.

The government can't publish the real rate of inflation as their official rate because then everyone would be demanding that percentage amount of increase in their pay, in both government and all other jobs. Actually, it is a good thing that the reported rate is lower because if the actual rate were reported there would be a stampede by employees to get higher pay in line with inflation, which would have the effect of increasing inflation even more. On top of this, inflation affects different people in different ways according to their lifestyle (vegetarians, for example, are not affected by an inflationary increase of price of meat because they do not buy meat). If inflation were reported as higher, it would cause the inflation to forcibly, and unfairly, affect everyone because all prices would automatically be put up by that amount each year. Finally, not having it reported as higher is beneficial to those who know what the true rate is because it allows them to act personally in a way to increase wealth that would not be possible to do if the true rate were reported.

Severe high inflation

While gradual, controlled inflation can be good; severe inflation, when the money loses its value very quickly and in a way that is out of control, is not. If too much money is printed, financial markets become awash with more money than services and this can be the start of severe inflation if not immediately checked by less printing, higher interest rates and restricted government spending.

At the heart of severe inflation is something called the "inflationary spiral." An inflationary spiral can be initiated in many ways, but one way is when there is a sudden large increase in money issued by a government. This large increase creates very quick inflation and higher prices for goods and services. Because the taxes are made up of this newly inflated money and do not, by the time of their collection, have enough value left for the government to use them, the government is forced to print even more money in order to run the country. This of course increases inflation even more and pushes the government into a cycle that is nearly impossible to stop. The inflation continues ever onward with the upward printing of currency and the downward value of the money in circulation. This type of inflationary spiral happened in Germany in the 1920s, in Eastern Europe in the 1990s, and in Zimbabwe in 2007. Severe high inflation in these cases was a destructive and heart-breaking experience for all those involved. The only way to stop an inflationary spiral after it has started is to replace the old money with completely different and new money— this is how the inflationary spiral in Germany was stopped. The way this is done is by exchanging in a very short period of time all the existing currency for a new currency (printing enough to satisfy the demand), after which very short period of time the old money is rendered by the government worthless and un-exchangeable for anything.

As mentioned, in Germany after World War I there occurred devastating inflation to the point that a person might be paid with a wheel barrow full of paper money in order to purchase a loaf of bread, and yet in order to take advantage of the value of that money, it would have to be spent right away. A student related to me an event that her father had recalled from that time. This student's father had gone for a walk in the German Alps, bordering Switzerland. On his outward journey in the morning he saw that he only had sufficient money to buy just one full meal at a passing restaurant, so he decided that it would be better to buy his meal on the way back during the late afternoon. Unfortunately, upon going to the restaurant later for his one meal of the day, the full meal that he had expected to purchase had almost doubled in price so that he had to buy a lesser meal and go hungry. He dared not wait to spend his money the next day because he knew that it would purchase even less.

Having done a good deal of volunteer work in Eastern Europe, I have seen first-hand the devastating effects of high inflation. In some of these countries inflation rates sometimes exceeded 50% per year and interest charges demanded by banks were in the order of 33% to 100% per year—which was necessary for the banks to survive and in order to run the economy.

In Bulgaria in the mid-1990s, inflation ranged from thirty-five percent to several hundred percent per year. This was due to the government (the individual people who were running the country) thinking that they could prevent the rising gasoline prices by mandating the fixed sale price of a liter of gasoline. While costs of oil went up and the value of the currency went down, there came a time when the gasoline could not be purchased and refined in Bulgaria for a price that allowed for the costs of its refinement, let alone to sell at the pump. The country was almost brought to an economic standstill. I happened to arrive on one of my volunteer assignments at the end of a ten-times depreciation of Bulgaria's currency against other Western European and U.S. currencies; it was a painful time for most people. I remember taking eight of my hosts out for an evening at a prestigious restaurant. Everyone thought that I was a millionaire because I told them to order what they liked without regard to the prices. I knew the exchange rate so I knew I could pay the bill, which came to U.S. $39, including the tip.

The biggest problem Bulgaria had at the time was that the country's productivity was very low in comparison with the rest of the world. When a country's average work output per person is low but government expenditures are high then there are inflationary pressures which are very hard to control. This is the type of thing that happened in each of these Eastern European countries after the collapse of Communism.

Before the collapse of Communism, a person in Russia might have been able to save 10,000 Rubles over a ten-year period to buy a Russian-made car. Within the space of the following six years after the collapse, that same 10,000 rubles had so depreciated in value that it could not buy even a cup of coffee. The government kept on adding zeroes to the currency as it was printed and the value kept going down.

This whole process was exacerbated by the fact that there was not enough work for the majority of the people, who had limited skills and training, which skills and training were neither required nor useful under the new free enterprise system. Many workers had been trained to do menial or repetitive work as the government required, but which had no value under a system of free enterprise. Many of the government enterprises were for products that were no longer needed. Skills to produce those things that *were* needed had to be learned, which is why the help they received from the West was so important. But these changes all took time, and so, during this transition period, there was the problem of low productivity in a country with high government expenditures.

Meanwhile, inflation was out of control and protective investment strategies for high inflation were not available because the communistic countries prior to 1988 did not believe in or allow personal ownership, let alone speculation for any wealth advancement, and this carried on in the minds of the people after the fall of communism. In time, policies and attitudes began to relax in respect to ownership of real property, but it happened slowly. In fact, the process to free up the land and property to be given or sold to individuals and corporations is still going on, and is likely to take many more years. Consequently, the idea that anyone could invest what they had so they could protect what they earned from inflation was not there, making the situation ultimately worse.

Protecting your assets from inflation

Knowing how to protect your assets against inflation is very important. At a prestigious gated community I know there is a unique mix of residents who have "made it," yet I have seen some who, having "made it," find that after a few years they can no longer afford to live in that community because the maintenance and other fees keep moving inexorably upwards. These otherwise smart business people put their well-earned retirement nest egg into a 100% "safe place" like annuities, corporate bonds, government bonds and tax-free bonds to ensure it remained safe. A "guaranteed" income from the interest was assured—or so they believed. The problem that developed, slowly but surely, was that the real value of their investment income became increasingly insufficient to meet the slowly but surely increasing costs of living. While the association and club fees doubled in ten years, their assets and income did not.

Investing long term in fixed-asset securities is, historically, the most unsafe way to safeguard your assets, though you may be told otherwise. Just look at the $1,000 railway bonds sold in the 1890s as a prudent investment with maturity in 100 years. $1,000 would purchase a lot in the 1890s, when a dollar-a-day wage was a very fine income for a worker. It was worth at least four years' wages. And what would each $1,000 bond be worth 100 years later, in the 1990's when a General Motors worker receives over a hundred times the amount in pay, or over $12,000 in wages and benefits per year? A 30-year government bond that you might purchase today for $100,000 is more than likely to have a real value at the end of 30 years of just $12,500 due to inflation. Likewise, the real value of the interest you receive, taxed or not, depreciates by a similar amount. The government uses the money you lend them and then pays you back in cheaper dollars, so you are in a sense paying the government in order to loan it money. Rather than being a "safe" investment, it's a guaranteed way to lose the value of your money.

Another guaranteed way to lose money is to put it under the mattress, or even into a bank account that pays interest, again all because of inflation. Inflation always erodes any kind of cash, whether in hand or in the bank. The money put into the bank will depreciate almost as fast as money under a mattress. Although in the bank you may be earning interest, it is important to know that no bank interest can compete with inflation if it is only simple payment of interest annually. It will not be able to beat inflation, let alone keep up with it. And besides all this, you have to pay taxes on the interest you get from the bank, making the situation even worse.

Some acquaintances of mine sold their homes and put most of the money into an interest-paying savings account to keep it "safe" preparatory to buying another home. They waited for a while, thinking that in time they would be able to find a lower-priced home. However, within three years they found that the value of their money had so lowered their purchasing power and the price of homes so increased that they could no longer afford to buy a home at all. The decisions they had made, both to put the money in the bank and to wait to buy another house, were disastrous for their future financial well-being, mainly because their ability to generate income had changed. They could not get a mortgage from a bank because the banks did not believe that they had, with their income, the financial ability to regularly make payments for such a high value type of loan.

So how do we protect our assets from inflation rather than doing the reverse? There has to be a way to protect money long term from inflation, even for those who don't like to worry about financial matters. Luckily there is.

When trying to protect your money against the effects of inflation it is important to place any surplus money into areas of growth. High-interest bonds and other fixed-income methods as previously mentioned do not give good protection from inflation, but there are certain areas that have proven historically to do so. If you are younger, then the long-term investment of your money in a diversified portfolio of stocks from the S&P 500 is one of the best ways to protect your money from inflation, and this option gives you the most flexibility (this type of investing is covered extensively in the long-term investing chapter). Such long-term investment offers steady gains in value at pace with or greater than inflation, and has the added benefit of supplementing your income through dividends. Also, you get the flexibility of being able to take out money from the portfolio without having necessarily to sell any of your holdings. This is especially valuable if the market happens to be down and you need money, because it means you won't have to sell in the down market in order to get that cash.

The Ibbotson reports show that the doubling of the average price of stocks over an extended period of time (like ten years) has proven to be a consistent trend in the history of the stock market. If you find that this has not happened for a certain good quality stock, you will almost certainly find that the company has given a stock split at some point in time. (A stock split is when a company will issue, for example, two company shares to replace every one company share that is then currently on the market, so that now there are two shares that are each at half the price of what the previous one share was worth.) In this case, while the stock price might not have doubled, there would now be ownership of twice as many shares. Thus the stock in real terms has still increased in value significantly.

When using this strategy of long-term investing, it is important to get only the highest quality stocks that pay regular dividends. Such stocks should not include those that constantly go up and down in price, or specialty stocks that tend to come and go with customer sentiment, such as restaurant chains, apparel chains, and transport industry. You should not have any trouble doing this because there are quite a few good, well-run companies that overall have a great history of paying regular dividends. One that comes quickly to mind is Archer Daniels Midland who, up to the time of writing, has not missed the paying of a quarterly dividend for eighty years or more, and has had several stock splits. The foregoing does not mean that there are not some cyclical stocks that can do well, it is only that trading such shares falls into the area of short-term trading—buying lower and selling higher—which is not a simple a thing for those not used to doing it (more on short- term investing is covered in a later chapter).

For those who are already retired, however, putting money into the stock market is likely *not* the best solution. This is because those who are retired do not have the luxury of time to see an investment rise in value over a long period, and putting money into the market for a short period of time would be too risky. However, if you know you will be around for at least seven to ten years, then history has shown that, after such a time, a group of diversified, dividend-paying stocks will, on average, rise at or above inflation.

Buying a rental property and then renting it out is the next best way to protect your money from inflation. Property values have always appreciated in line with inflation, and so your money will be protected when invested in that way. In addition, the rent paid by the tenants (which also goes up with inflation) will likely bring in sufficient income to pay the expenses of ownership of the property (such as expenses for upkeep and maintenance) and perhaps even the monthly payments to the bank if you bought the property on a loan. And as time progresses the burden of such payments will become easier because the value of the property and your income from it will go up because of inflation, but the mortgage payments you have to make will stay relatively the same.

The ideal situation would be to buy on terms (like a mortgage) a single building with four or eight apartments (a four-plex or eight-plex). Of course there would be some level of regular maintenance, and to deal with this, you might employ the services of a rental agency. Their charges generally equal about 7% of the rental income, which I have found to be well worth the cost. Such rental agencies are made up of professionals who know how to prevent the moving in of people you don't want—those who would not pay the rent or who would cause above- average damage to the property. Although one cannot expect to get a high dividend to begin with because of the initial expenses involved, having your own rental property protects the value of your invested money from inflation, gives you a regular income by way of rent that also goes up with inflation, and finally—If you wanted to—you could live in one of your apartments essentially rent free.

If you were looking for something still further to protect your money from inflation, another possibility would be to invest in a piece of land that was not too far outside an expanding city. While all land generally appreciates at the same rate as inflation, there is a much greater appreciation in areas that are near cities or industry where there will be further expansion of society.

The importance of productivity

One reason for inflation, as previously mentioned, is man's tendency to avoid productivity but to be paid more nevertheless, thus de-valuing the money which is based on the work they do. Low average productivity equals a poor standard of living, higher inflation, and decreased purchasing power by that country's currency. We have all seen ants at work—what would happen if they stopped? They would all die, and the truth is that the same thing would happen to us, the human race, if we all stopped working and became non-productive. Good productivity is the key to higher currency values, lower inflation, and a higher standard of living.

Poor productivity is why, during the 1950s, the English currency went down significantly against other currencies, as high inflation took away the accumulated wealth of hundreds of thousands of people. The wartime savings bonds sold by the government to assist in the war effort against Germany became almost worthless in comparison to their original investment. How did this all happen? After the Second World War was over, there was a great resurgence of the Labor Party, who promised to give the returned soldiers better wages and conditions. The new Labor Party did not like the key industries of England being run by big businesses, including transportation, utilities, and coal. They believed that big businesses were ruthless and unfair to their workers, and they thought that the profits made could be better distributed to the workers if the government controlled them, just like in Russia. After all, it was the workers who did the work in these large enterprises, and therefore they deserved more and better pay.

And so it was thought that the workers should be given more money and should work fewer hours, with more annual holidays each year. Combined with this, a new health scheme was launched which would give everyone free access to the entire healthcare of the nation. The radical unions were very much pro-Russian and because of what they promised they were very popular with the workers. The end result was that the government of the day started to nationalize all that they could, by forcing the coal, transportation, and utility companies to sell to the government all of their assets (at a price considerably less than the assets were worth, too).

Of course, it was necessary to fund all of the purchasing that was being done by the government. The only way that they could do so was to print more money—and a great deal of it, too! This, combined with the lower productivity, created very high inflation. Things seemed to go well for the first eighteen months, but after that the situation started to go downhill fast. Managers were appointed who were not qualified to run the various industries at a profit—after all, why make a profit if you knew that there was plenty of money available from the government? Service, reliability, and productivity sank lower and lower in all sectors as prices moved higher and higher. A worker who was inefficient or broke the basic rules of employment was difficult to fire. The unions would not allow any worker to suffer in the least and would threaten to go on strike at the slightest complaint. As prices rose, the unions demanded more pay and would strike if higher wages were not granted. They did not understand how the economy worked. In any case, each worker was required to pay their union dues—which were supposed to be for their future benefit, and went into a fund to help operate the union, such as to pay union employees and union expenses. However, the increasing costs and depreciating value of union funds, all due to inflation, wasted much of what was contributed by the union members. The various industries became non-competitive and the beginning of an inflationary spiral started.

The coal mining industry and railways became the most inefficient, and as a result their prices went up. This affected the export of goods, which became less desirable for companies outside of England to buy because they could get the product more cheaply from other countries. Surpluses built up because the cost of getting it to market was considerably greater than that for which the product could be sold.

Fortunately, this state of affairs in England did not last too long. Even so, the severe inflation caused by the policies of the British Labor Party in the 1950s caused a lot of pain to many people—especially those on fixed pensions.

Could severe inflation happen in the United States? Certainly it could, though it is unlikely in the short term. All it would take would be for us as individuals to vote in and sustain a government that promised us that which the government could not afford without printing more paper money and who could not—or would not—provide the work to back it. It would take a government that offered a great deal for free and required nothing in return. "Vote for me," such a candidate might say, "and I will guarantee that everyone, from the time they enter the workplace, gets a full adult wage—no more sweated labor for our youth. Everyone will get five weeks paid holiday and two weeks accumulated paid sick leave each year. Three months paid long service leave every seven years. We will tax the rich to make life more equitable for everyone. We will look after the poor. Free comprehensive unlimited medical treatment as well as payments to support your children. Full, livable wages if you lose your job. Good retirement pensions for all—no one need want ever again."

I do not think that the intelligence of the American people would fall for such a myth. If a few of these promises, let alone the whole of them, were carried out, it would send the economy into a downturn that would eventually cause it to severely falter. Inflation would escalate, businesses would not take risks to grow and expand or employ more labor—especially young, unskilled labor. Our economy would be put into such a tailspin that it would lower everyone's standard of living and erode, if not exhaust, most people's previously built up savings. All those promises sound nice to those who want to be "treated right" and be looked after, but that is not what life is about. You can't really get something for nothing. And even if you could, I am convinced that it would not be good for man's individual progress.

Unfortunately, this type of thinking happened in Australia in the mid-1970s. In 1973 I exchanged some Australian dollars and received US $1.46 for each. The value of the Australian dollar after that almost exactly reversed for a time and remained devalued for more than thirty years. What happened was that the Australian electorate was promised "the good life" and paid for it with higher inflation and a lower standard of living for two decades. Australia is blessed with being a naturally rich country in its own right—gold, iron ore, coal, renewable resources, as well as agriculture production that abounds in great quantity. Such a country is hard to keep down. Yet starting in the mid-1970s it has not been a good place for businesses and industry, especially from overseas, because of the labor laws and high taxes due, for the most part, to the mentality I have described.

I lived in Australia for 20 years, in the 50s and 60s, and was sad to see it lose a great deal of its fine heritage. Many professionals who had worked hard all their lives and saved to get more money found that they were not entitled to an old age pension or other benefits because of the amount of their assets, which they had worked hard for, whereas people who had worked less and spent their money, thus having less in savings and assets, were entitled to all the benefits such as free transport, old age pension, retirement entitlements, etc. In this case those who worked hard were poorly rewarded, financially speaking, for their past achievements. Even today, everyone is asked questions to determine how many assets they have before they are allowed a pension, and if they have income or assets beyond a certain amount they will not qualify. Meanwhile, those who have deliberately "worked the system" for government handouts will easily get a pension.

The good news is that if you live there now, it is climbing out of its failed social experiment and is on the road to recovery. Things are beginning to change, and life for the average person there is relatively good. Indeed, Australia, currently, is a great place to live. Many people take advantage of a SUB economy, that is, a CASH economy—people paying back and forth in cash only, in order to escape paying the high taxes, which form a disincentive for working more than is necessary in a regular job. The cash economy enables many people to live quite well, and gives them an incentive to work hard for it.

Taking advantage of inflation

The U.S. government can make a very good financial deal when borrowing money—the issuing and selling of government bonds. By creating these bonds, the government takes advantage of the way inflation works. Of course, the amount of money that the government borrows has to be paid back sometime, even if it has to be borrowed again. However, unlike other debtors, governments can take a double bite out of the money they borrow—firstly by its natural devaluation over time due to inflation (meaning that when the government finally pays back the bond it is worth in real terms significantly less than the

24

amount they borrowed originally), and, secondly, by *taxing* the interest that they pay out to the lender and the holders of the government bonds, thus getting some of it back. It works roughly like this: The government borrows $20 million by issuing bonds at, say, 6 1/4% per year for a ten-year maturity. Each year their real payments, after they get money back from the tax on the interest, is nearer to 4 1/2%. Over a ten-year period the government pays 10 x 4 1/2% interest on $20 million = $9 million. There is also the payback of the $20 million at the end of ten years, which can be printed or borrowed again. But because the value of money has approximately halved by that time, due to inflation, the payback is really only $10 million in original value. They have actually *made* $10 million ($20 million borrowed but only $10 million in real worth paid back—equals $10 million in their pockets)!

It's a very good deal. They borrow high-value money, and pay back with cheaper money. They use the extra money, which costs them effectively nothing, to spend in any way they want. This is the only good business deal that the government can make, though somewhat unwittingly against itself because it steals *value* from the very population that elected them. Incidentally many of us take advantage of this phenomenon when we take out a mortgage or long-term loan to buy a house, property, or anything else that historically and steadily goes up in price over time. We borrow money while we are younger, on terms, and then wait until a later time, by which time our property has gone up while our payments have gone down, and we are finally able to sell what we purchased, if we want to, at the higher price.

I have purchased or built several homes in my lifetime, and usually I have borrowed money from a bank or mortgage lender in order to pay for them. As an example, if I purchased a home for $100,000 and put down a deposit of $20,000 and borrowed the other $80,000, then sold the home twenty years later for $400,000 (equal to my estimated rate of inflation of about 7.2% compounded annually) I would realize a gain of $300,000 on what I had purchased the home for. Even though this money is worth less due to inflation, yet because I only put down a deposit of $20,000, my actual profit would be, in real terms, at least five times my original investment (if the

$300,000 is only worth $100,000 in real terms after figuring in inflation, then that is still 5 times my original down payment of $20,000), and all because I would have borrowed high-cost money and paid it back in cheaper money! I have of course oversimplified this because there are many other factors to be taken into account. However, buying property in this manner can be a very good way of gaining later wealth, and all because of inflation.

You might think that the banks lose money, but they do not. The banks are in the fortunate position of being able to use accumulations of relatively small deposits for lending out at longer terms, and it is here that they make their real money. They utilize all the money they can (even that which isn't really theirs) towards getting interest. If you were to put $100 in your account today without interest, tomorrow or even the same day the bank would be utilizing it to good advantage by lending the money out to others; it matters not that you take your $100 out tomorrow, because others would have put money in. This is only one of the ways that banks can do very well from their depositors. And this is as it should be. After all, banks have expenses and shareholders just like any other company and they deserve to be recompensed according to their services. If they couldn't make money, then the banks would not exist and the valuable service they perform would not be available.

Conclusion

There is no doubt in my mind that some level of inflation is beneficial for the average person. If dealt with properly, inflation can give us a sense of wellbeing in that we can expect to get some level of increased wealth in the future, as long as we know how inflation works. When properly leveraged, inflation has the ability to take what we own now and increase its real value later in our lives. However, we are never far away from the risk of above normal inflation, especially with the tendency of some politicians to give people for free what they ought to be working for. Inflation can be like fire, a good friend and a bad enemy. Good because it takes us into increased wealth.

Bad because, taken beyond a certain point, the increased wealth becomes an illusion.

Inflation has been around as long as there has been a monetary system, hundreds, perhaps thousands, of years. As to its cause, on top of what has been mentioned, there are complicating factors not even wholly understood by economists and clearly not well understood by politicians, who so often are unaware of the damage that can be caused by overspending or by restricting personal initiative. We are not likely to ever permanently get rid of the slow and steady erosion of money values. However, to keep it within reasonable bounds is essential. Never forget that the real value of money is the work that is behind it.

EXTRA: Story of the Three Brothers

The following story is an illustration of how important it is to be aware of inflation. It shows how three people, starting with the same sum of money, can end up with vastly different results.

There were three brothers, who were each left a sizable sum of money by their grandfather at his death. Indeed, he left them each $500,000. The first brother was ultra conservative. He went to his bank manager and asked which investment would guarantee the safety of the principle of his inheritance of $500,000. "Well," said the manager, "we have a particularly great ten-year fixed rate certificate of deposit that pays a 6 1/2% annual interest. It is very safe, as the government guarantees the principle. You therefore cannot lose your money, and you will also get $32,500 each year for the life of the CD" (Certificate of Deposit) "Great," said the first brother. "I will take it and invest my inheritance in the CD that you suggest!"

The second brother was less conservative. He decided to make his own investment by buying some property. He felt that his future could be assured if he purchased a four-plex, apartment building. He could live in one apartment and rent the other three. He did just that and used his $500,000 to pay for the four-plex.

The third brother was adventurous. He decided that he would like to purchase and run a hotel/motel. However he found that his inheritance was not sufficient to buy one as the prices for good properties in the right location were too high. Nevertheless, he made an offer of $2,000,000 on a $2,200,000 property that was up for sale, subject only to his being able to obtain the necessary financing. He was able to obtain the financing easily as his deposit was substantial, being equal to twenty five percent of the purchase price ($500,000). Also he would be intimately involved in the operation of the new enterprise. His offer was accepted.

The First Brother

After just one year, the first brother received his $32,500 interest. His principle was intact, yet the purchasing power of his $500,000, in the bank, had been reduced by $25,000 due to inflation so that it was worth some less. Yet he was not particularly aware of it. He had his income of $32,500 from the bank and led a contented trouble-free existence.

Unfortunately, the Internal Revenue Service considered his $32,500 to be unearned income, it being interest from an investment, so the total amount of taxes was $5,000 after his allowances. This was painful, but not disastrous.

His end-of-year position was therefore: $500,000 original investment + $32,500 interest for the past year = $532,500, minus $25,000 to factor in inflation and $5,000 so taxes, leaving him, in real terms, with $502,000.

Now inflation, or the loss of purchasing power, equals about 7% each year compounded yearly (as is covered on the chapter on money and inflation). Hence the first brother, instead of living off his interest income, may eventually have to keep his old job or get outside employment, assuming he does not delve into his capital. We will assume that he does not want to spend any of the original inheritance money but just lets it remain in the bank. It should be noted that his original deposit will continue to show up on his bank statements as $500,000, not as the amounts detailed below. But the deposit will continue to have reduced purchasing power. These real values are shown below for the first through twelfth year.

Start of Year	Value of Original Deposit
FIRST YEAR	$500,000
SECOND YEAR	$465,000
THIRD YEAR	$432,450
FOURTH YEAR	$402,178
FIFTH YEAR	$374,026
SIXTH YEAR	$347.844
SEVENTH YEAR	$323,495
EIGHTH YEAR	$300,850
NINTH YEAR	$279,790
TENTH YEAR	$260,205
ELEVENTH YEAR	$241,991
TWELFTH YEAR	$225,051
TWENTIETH YEAR	$125,934
FORTIETH YEAR	$33,161
EIGHTIETH YEAR	$2,072

It can be seen that it is never a viable option to invest in a CD at a bank or other institution on a long-term basis—at any rate of interest. Roughly speaking, prices double, or the value of money halves, every ten years or so in the United States. In most other countries, the rate of inflation is even higher. If I decided to extend the above time out to the fortieth year, which comes to $33,161, or to eighty years, halving the amount every ten years, the end result is terrible as to the real spending value.

So the first brother, after twelve years, had lost nearly half of his inheritance in original purchasing power due to the somewhat benign 7% annual compounded inflation. I say benign, because we do not see it in the short-term, and for many of us, if we do not see it, then it's not there! Certainly the figures look terrible; however I am old enough to remember that my mother purchased a home for $500 in

1930 which could now be sold for around $500,000, or around one thousand times the original purchase price. Yes 1,000 times, and not percent!

My personal estimate of the real average of all around inflation is in the region of 7.2%, compounded annually. It becomes self-evident that after thirty years the first brother would have very little left of his original inheritance, certainly not enough to live on in his later life. His social security might not be very high either, because most of his income, if only from the interest on the CD, would not have required social security payments.

The Second Brother

The second brother put himself in a better position than the first. Remember he had decided to purchase a four-plex apartment block. He had paid cash for it which had enabled him to negotiate a better purchase price.

At the end of his first year his position was as follows: The four-plex had appreciated at 7% (or the inflation rate) as property does, and was therefore now worth (if he were interested in selling it) $535,000. His net income, after all repairs, taxes and operating expenses from renting the other three apartments was $42,800. It therefore gave him an 8% return on his investment. Additionally he was able to have his own accommodation more or less free of charge. We must not forget the taxes on his net income of $42,800, which amount would have been $8,560, if his tax rate was the same as his first brother. We will assume that he spent his earned income after taxes and did not put any of it towards his capital. His normal maintenance could have helped appreciate his property nevertheless. The table below shows the appreciated value of his four-plex over time.

Year	Value of Original Deposit

FIRST YEAR	$535,000
SECOND YEAR	$572,450
THIRD YEAR	$612,522
FOURTH YEAR	$655,398
FIFTH YEAR	$701,275
SIXTH YEAR	$750,364
SEVENTH YEAR	$802,891
EIGHTH YEAR	$859,092
NINTH YEAR	$919,230
TENTH YEAR	$983,576
ELEVENTH YEAR	$1,052,424
TWELFTH YEAR	$1,126,096
TWENTIETH YEAR	$1,934,842

This is the amount at which he could sell his property for after twenty years, if inflation continued at the same rate, and I am being conservative if you consider the steady climb of property values over many a previous twenty-year period.

Now we should consider his income over that same period. Unlike simple interest, which is not subject to any inflationary pressure, income is. Rent has a tendency to climb steadily over time.

Having received $42,000 during his first year of renting, based on the same formula used for the capital appreciation, his final year's income at the end of the sixth year would be $53,603 and at the twelfth year $71,833. Of course in real terms he would not be much better off, because he is only keeping up with the increasing cost of living. However, even this is a plus for anyone.

It becomes clear, that the second son did quite well with his somewhat conservative investment and could look forward to a reasonable standard of living in his retirement.

The Third Brother

Now let us look at the last brother, who, quite adventurously, decided to purchase a motel/hotel complex with a down payment of

$500,000, leaving a borrowed balance of $1,500,000 that drew an interest payment of 8% per annum.

Because of its size and also that he was prepared to act as manager, he was able to make a net profit after all expenses of 8% on the value of the hotel/motel complex. The complex had cost $2,000,000 so that his profit at the end of the first year was $160,000. Remember that his own funds which he had put into the enterprise was just $500,000. His gross profit was therefore a whopping 32% on his original investment. Not bad at all! However we must not forget the Tax Man, who this time took 35% of his $160,000 net business profit, or $56,000, which left him with a net profit balance of only $104,000. Still very good after tax and all expenses.

At the end of his first year, because of the aforementioned inflationary pressure, his hotel/motel now had a value of $2,118,811; at the end of the second year it was $2,267,128!

Year	Value of Building
FIRST YEAR END	$2,140,000
SECOND YEAR END	$2,289,000
THIRD YEAR.	$2,450,086
FOURTH YEAR	$2,621,592
FIFTH YEAR	$2,805,103
SIXTH YEAR	$3,001,461
SEVENTH YEAR	$3,211,563
EIGHTH YEAR	$3,436,372
NINTH YEAR	$3,676,918
TENTH YEAR	$3,934,303
ELEVENTH YEAR	$4,209,704
TWELFTH YEAR	$4,504,383
TWENTIETH YEAR	$7,739,369

Of course the above figures are based on the long-term average inflation rate of 7%, which might be higher or lower in any period of time. But it matters not, because the relative purchasing power and values remain the same. Real values go hand in hand with inflation eventually, even if they are sometimes skewed out of position.

And so you can see that out of all three brothers, the third brother fared the best, and also was the one who was the most involved in his business. Being money smart and taking action gave him two big advantages.

Perhaps I have taken some liberty with the numbers. Nevertheless, the above examples show the true trends of each investment, which each start with the same value. However, I don't recommend that any of the above be practiced by you, the reader, should you find yourself left with a large inheritance. Your age, work abilities, and risk tolerances would greatly affect where you should invest. However, the example of the brothers is a good one for understanding how it is necessary to be wise with your money and invest in such a way as to keep inflation in check.

CHAPTER TWO

Money Management: How to Handle Your Money

If you are like 95% of all people younger than 35, your money management has been limited to seeing how much you have left in your account at the bank, what your credit card account balances are, and waiting to pay your current and upcoming bills from your next paycheck. Perhaps you are not certain you can pay all of your bills this month.

If all seems well with your accounts, you might feel it's all right to go and splurge a little. Perhaps you have been hoping to buy something new, or to have a decent holiday, or perhaps you would like to enjoy dinner out with friends. Afterwards, when an unexpected bill comes in, you have to do some juggling to pay it. You may then be inclined to think, "If I only had more money, then all would be well!" Has your life always seemed to run along these lines? Yet more money is rarely the answer; it's what you do with what you get that makes the difference.

I am not entirely against spending. I am just against spending money that you do not have. Even spending money that you an-ticipate getting but have not received is a recipe for trouble. Spending your next paycheck immediately when you get it and living from hand to mouth can be very wearing and will ultimately detract from your mental well-being. Your life will continue to be rudderless unless you decide *you* are going to be in control. Instead of your money—or lack of it—ruling you, you should rule it! When that happens you will find it possible to do things you never could have imagined doing before. You will be able to look forward to quality living, no matter what income you get. You will save and get out of debt so that you can move forward with your life and anticipate good things in the future, notwithstanding any changes in your financial circumstances. With less financial stress the chances are that you will live a longer, more satisfying life.

One of the problems we humans have is that we want more, not less. We get used to our normal way of living, and we think we have to have what we are used to. We say that we are poor when we cannot have everything we want. Most of us do not know the meaning of the word 'poor'. We don't know what it's like to go hungry or worry about where we are going sleep at night. We may worry about how much food is on our table, rather than if it's there at all. We want cars for every driving member of our family. We give our children the things they want so they will be happy. The minute our furniture begins to look faded and worn, we feel we must replace it. Or perhaps we feel we must keep up appearances for our friends and neighbors. This is the spending that perpetually keeps us *'poor'*!

Perhaps we feel poor because we are earning minimum wage or are using government or other assistance and cannot buy what others are buying. But do we really have to have our daily beer and cigarettes? Do we really have to go out for fast food? Or a night out? Or buy more clothes so that we will look better? Do we want today what we cannot afford? We certainly won't be able to afford it in the future if we aren't smart with our finances now.

I have heard it reported that 76% of all women and a little less of all men are chronic, compulsive buyers. At the same time it was reported that these compulsive buyers have limited incomes. This is not a new phenomenon. In the 1700s and 1800s, both in England and America, debtors' prisons were overflowing with people who could not pay what they owed, and they stayed there until they or their family paid up. Many people of all ages do not understand the importance of being careful with money and having a budget.

A budget is essential for your future financial well-being, and it's never too late to start. The first thing you need to do is to run a simple monthly forward budget that plans at least nine months into the future.

To set up the type of budget you will need to write it down, either on paper or on your computer. Use a method where you can easily make changes. It is likely to take you at least one hour to work out a reasonably good budget, depending on the complexity of your household finances. It will be natural to make some mistakes to begin with; don't worry about this. The point here is to learn what you earn and spend, and to train yourself to follow a plan. Within the first month you will be able to make the adjustments to keep you on track for the following months.

Expenses

To begin with, you should put down all of the essential expenses that you have to pay each month. All the budgeted expenses must be put into categories. These can be divided into component parts like this:

Food expense (month on average)	Monthly $?
(Later you can divide by four to give you a rough idea of what you can afford to spend each week)	
Rent or mortgage	Monthly $?
Electric power	Monthly $?
Water and sewer	Monthly $?
Telephone	Monthly $?
Car payments and operation, gas etc.	Monthly $?
All insurance payments	Monthly $?
All other essential family payments	Monthly $?
Necessary clothing	Monthly $?
Medical expenses or insurance	Monthly $?
Bank interest and charges	Monthly $?
All credit card interest & penalties	Monthly $?
Credit card payments	Monthly $?
(plus 10% of the outstanding balance, so you can start reducing your monthly total)	
Total of all	**Monthly $?**

Next you put what might be called discretionary items, or nonessential expenses, which you may or may not buy. Discretionary spending is where you can make a decision whether to spend or not.

These include:

Gasoline	Monthly $?
Entertainment (such as movies)	Monthly $?
Dinners out	Monthly $?
Parties	Monthly $?
Gifts to others	Monthly $?
Church and other charitable donations	Monthly $?
Impulse buying such as snacks	Monthly $?
Merchandise at stores and street vendors	Monthly $?
Repairs & renewals to property you have	Monthly $?
Holidays and vacations	Monthly $?
Special occasions	Monthly $?
Weddings and birthdays	Monthly $?
Family clothing and school supplies	Monthly $?
Tuition	Monthly $?

(*Note: For anything that is not paid monthly (but rather, quarterly or annually, such as Taxes) you still need to make a monthly allowance. In order to do this, you estimate what it will cost on a yearly basis, then divide by twelve in order to enter it as an average monthly expense. Once the money is ear-marked for the various items, it is no longer available to spend on any other item. You have to be firm with this!*)

The next category necessary to consider is something called contingencies. Contingency planning is a must-have in any budget. Contingencies are those expenses that cannot be planned for. These include unexpected events such as loss of employment, reduced income, a general change of circumstances, accident, sickness, or even death. Of course it's impossible to know what problems may come our way, but it's nevertheless necessary for us to be prepared financially for such things, because they will happen sooner or later, make no mistake. None of us can predict the future, but we know that Illness, death, fire and injury can and do occur constantly, and we see it reported in the news all the time. If we are wise, we will set aside an allowance for such unexpected events.

So how do we allow for contingencies? One way is to divide the total of *all* expenses by 100 then multiply by 112 to get a 12% con-tingency allowance on all of your expenses each month. This amount needs to be put in a separate savings account. It is then set aside and cannot be spent in any other way. Monthly contingency amounts should always be carried forward for twelve months. In other words, the contingency account should be built up for twelve months, after which you no longer need to add to it, unless you deplete the reserve due to some event, in which case you need to build it up to the twelve month amount again. Any surplus can be used for investment, but whatever amount is expended for an emergency should be made up again as soon as possible.

Total expenses	**Monthly $?**
Contingency allowance 12%	Monthly $?
Grand Total of all possible expenses	*Monthly $?*

Saving for a rainy day

It is always a good idea to have some reserve, either in cash or in your ability to borrow money for some future need. That need might be education, a new car, or a medical emergency. The list is endless. For example, you may be young and on a roll, but what would happen if you were laid off and your income suddenly dried up? Do you have any reserves? Take steps right now to build up some savings. Even if you are in a good place and have lots of income, you never know what will happen in the future, and it is best to be prepared.

There comes a time in each of our lives when an opportunity arises and we say, "If only I were able to take advantage of it!" This is another reason to have reserves. I recognized in my youth that there were many opportunities out there but they were no good to me unless I had the money to take advantage of them. Because of this, I decided to build up my own nest egg and joined the British army in 1947 in order to do so. At the end of my service an opportunity did present itself, and because of my nest egg I was able to start on the first leg of my business career.

Income

Now we get to the income side, which should be simple.

Your regular income	Monthly $?
All other income, from whatever source	Monthly $?
Total income =	Monthly $?
Subtract the grand total of all expenses	Monthly $?
Your surplus (or deficit)	Monthly $?

This surplus or deficit should be carried over to the next month, for which month you again tally up all of your expected expenses and income in the same way as described, to come up with another surplus or deficit which is again carried over to the next month. This should be done for nine months into the future. It will very quickly become evident if you are progressively accumulating a surplus or going the other way.

Hopefully you will find after completing your 9 month forward budget that you have a surplus. This then becomes what is called "disposable income." This discretionary amount of money is for your future well-being and not to spend on things that just have a temporary life. At least 90% of this disposable balance should be kept for future investments and savings. You have already taken care of all the various needs and most of the wants, like vacations etc. The surplus can therefore increase your long-term investments, whether they are in property, land, or the stock market—the list might be extensive. Using your surplus in this way is good because budgeting for investments on a monthly basis is not always possible, due to the normal variability of expenses and income, especially if you are tight on your finances.

Now, what if you are on the wrong side? Suppose that the total expenses consistently exceed the total income. What should you do? It is self-evident that, if you find at the end of each month that you have a cash deficit, then you need to reduce your expenses to bring them into line. It just has to be done, because the alternative will mean that you accumulate a larger and larger deficit, putting your financial future in ruins. Of course, if you have a deficit only because of non-essential payments, then it can be carried over to the next month as long as those less-urgent expenses are eventually paid off. Another way to fix a deficit might be to get another part-time job to give you more income.

If you find that instead of a surplus there is a deficit, it will quickly become apparent to you why you are always living from hand to mouth. You may always be trying to find ways to get additional money, and the cycle seems never to end. This is because you are spending more than you bring in. It's a battle that will never be won unless you take charge of where the money goes! Each family will be different, with different circumstances applying to them; however, it's always necessary to get to a position where the outgoings are at least in balance with the income. At that stage it is possible to make headway on the long-term financial security that you seek. Therefore, you need to examine each item in each category and decide what can be pared and by how much. This is something only you can do. I can point out some of the ways that you can economize, but only you can identify what applies to your particular circumstances. Not all of the items will be applicable to your lifestyle.

You may be very poor or very rich for differing reasons. Yet if you are unhappy with the way life is treating you due to financial burdens, now is the time for you to begin to get a handle on these problems. Life is meant to be a joyous experience. Yet to have that joy it is necessary to learn, and sometimes the learning is painful; thus the truism there is no gain without some pain. It may not be easy to lessen your spending, but in order to get a grip on your finances it is absolutely necessary. Let us look at the various ways money can be saved. They are not in any deliberate order of importance:

Food and clothing: Food is an essential item, yet it does not have to be expensive. For example, you can buy the same product for less by buying a different brand. Often the same original producer of a food item will put their product into several different companies' labels, and the price of those different labels may vary even though it is the same product. By consistently buying the cheaper label, it could easily mean a variation of $15 in every $100 spent. Another thing to be aware of when trying to save money on food is that eating more calories than are expended each week not only has a health consequence, but also a monetary consequence.

I have a friend who saved food money by memorizing what items should cost. Then she went to several stores, comparing and buying the cheapest items in each, because each store charges a slightly different amount. Many frugal shoppers also avail themselves of coupons and sales.

As for clothing, you need not buy new. There are good looking and serviceable clothes for all ages that can be purchased at thrift stores for a fraction of the cost of the same items new. Discount stores and clearance racks are also a great option for saving.

Utilities: Utilities have to be paid because they are necessities, and if you do not pay them they will be denied to you. However, you can make the effort to reduce where and when possible. Air conditioning can be adjusted to a higher temperature in the summer and heating to a lower temperature in the wintertime. By doing this you should be able to lower the bill by at least 25%.

Leaving lights or fans off when not needed can also be of great help towards reducing your electricity bill. Make sure that there is no wastage of water either.

Phones are counted as essential in most households. The technology is changing very fast, and the costs keep going down. Cell phone packages vary widely. There are even other options such as calling cards or Internet Protocol (VOIP). Do your research and choose the best plan for your needs—not your wants. For instance, you might need a cellphone for a child when they leave home to attend an activity, but that doesn't mean they need unlimited talk, text and data, or constant access to it.

Insurance: It is a good thing to have insurance for short periods of one's life, when there is some perceived danger or where it is necessary because of the law. But you should only have as much as is needed and not more.

One way to save money, in the case of car insurance, is to have several vehicles insured with the same insurance company which will allow the company to give you a better rate. This is because the risk of their paying out for each of the insured vehicles is significantly reduced. Another action you can take to save money is to have comprehensive insurance only on new or fairly new vehicles and otherwise just have third party insurance policies. Also, on new cars or valuable used cars, after time has passed, you can request a rate change based on the depreciated value of the vehicle. Once I insured a new vehicle for a moderate premium. After four years I requested a rate change to reflect the considerable depreciated value and requested it to be insured for only third party (generally, this is a state minimum requirement). The new premium was about one third less.

Where other insurances are concerned, such as life, property, and personal items, I have found over a lifetime that only when you feel very strongly that there is some risk of early demise, damage, or loss should insurance be considered. Insurance agents are adept at giving good advice for insurance that is the least cost to you. However insurance with some kind of annuity payout in your later life is generally a waste of your money. This is because the payouts, while seeming to be adequate, will not seem adequate later, due to the depreciating value of money and length of time involved! Having a contingency saving account for small loss and damage will save you money in the long run.

Interest payments: Interest payments have to be met, otherwise the lenders will cut off your ability to borrow, and in the worst scenario, foreclose on the debt. One way to reduce your interest payments is to renegotiate the loan so that your total interest and monthly repayments are lower. It is not recommended you do this unless you have to, because it means you pay more in the long run.

Another possibility is to consolidate all of your overdue accounts into equal monthly payments that you can manage. This is good if by doing so you can reduce the monthly interest payments you have to make (especially the high-interest accounts such as credit cards). However, consolidating your loans is a bad thing if the cost of consolidation and the length of time for repayments means you will pay considerably more than you already pay on your debt.

Finally, one way to reduce your interest payments on a loan with a high interest rate would be to take out a new loan against an asset that you have (your home or other security) at a lower interest rate and pay off the old loan with the new loan, thus replacing your high interest rate with a new, lower interest rate.

Credit Cards: Credit cards are like fire, a good friend and a bad enemy. If you are finding the monthly account gets out of hand, usually because of impulse buying, cut the cards up and throw them away. If you have a large amount of credit card debt, allow in your budget for 10% of your credit card account to be paid off every month until you can get to the point where you have eliminated it completely.

If you don't have enough income to pay off your credit card in this way, or if you can't completely pay it off in time, you must either re-negotiate your interest rate or declare bankruptcy. If you let the credit card companies know you are thinking of declaring bankruptcy, they are likely to be more willing to renegotiate your payments, because they would rather get something than nothing at all. It is also important that you make it clear how bad the situation really is.

Another thing you should do is start paying cash for everything—then you will think twice about paying out hard cash for that nice thing that takes your fancy. You should not buy items or services that you cannot afford, or have to go into debt for. Escaping today (by borrowing the money) only to face the music (or debt) tomorrow is not good sense. If you spend today, yet have worries tomorrow, it is surely counter-productive to your financial and emotional health.

Donations to organizations: We all like to give to those we feel in need, but what is the point if we then become one of the needy? We should not donate unless we can absolutely afford it and have no serious financial troubles of our own. I would say this also even if it were a religious donation. Unless that organization would help you financially or materially with food and clothing when you are in need, why pay a donation? Nevertheless, this is ultimately a personal thing.

Entertainment and parties: We all like to have friends and entertain them, yet this need not be with expensive and large amounts of food and drink. Having friends that like you for what you give them by way of material things, you can do without. If you cannot afford such entertainment, then you should not spend it to entertain others. What is the point of over spending now only to find that you are not able to pay essential bills later?

Unnecessary shopping and meals out: These items could be categorized under impulse buying. Impulse buying is, I think, the single most financially destructive habit that anyone can have. Here again, if you are locked into this habit, then put an amount into your budget beyond which you will not go and keep to it. If you are in financial trouble, it's best not to spend any money on these items at all, since they are not essential. But whatever you do, never use your credit card to go shopping for things that you do not need! A good practice is to wait two weeks before buying something you want. You may be surprised by how much less you want or even need that item, after you've had a little time to get used to going without it.

Property and other taxes: Property taxes can be a bind sometimes and they go up with the value of your property. The more your property goes up in value, the more taxes you will have to pay. Unfortunately, I have seen times when the enthusiasm of county property assessors assigned the property a higher value than what the property could be sold for. Challenging an appraisal can be daunting and very time consuming. However, if the property taxes are significantly beyond the value of the property, by challenging the assessors the value can be reassessed and the taxes thus lowered. Sometimes it is possible to send a written report as to why you wish to challenge the assessment. It is not uncommon to spend several days doing the research and attending hearings in order to accomplish this, so be prepared to put in some work if you decide to go this route.

You can get a fairly good idea if your property is assessed at too high a value by going to a realtor and asking what you could get for your property. If it is significantly less than what your property was assessed at, then this means your property was assessed too high.

Whatever you do, it is essential that you pay all your property and other taxes on time. If you do not pay all that is due on time, they will load the penalties onto you, and it is far more expensive to pay the penalties late than it is to pay on time.

Motor vehicle maintenance and repair: Motor vehicles need to be looked after and it is false economy to neglect them, although this is common practice. "I cannot afford to have the oil and filter changed every 3,000 miles," people say. But an ounce of prevention is worth a pound of cure. Buying a bomb of a vehicle because it is cheap and never fixing it up is false economy, because you will end up paying more in the end. I purchased several cheap motor vehicles in my younger years. However, I quickly learned to take any used vehicle immediately into a reputable service establishment to have a thorough service and maintenance checkup. Sure, it costs money to do so, but on balance it was less expensive than being stranded, or having constant breakdowns and endless repair expenses.

The way to handle a vehicle is to look after it. Always get the oil and filter changed regularly and have the standard 30, 60, and 90-thousand-mile services done at the correct time. If you give your motor vehicle tender loving care, over time you will save a considerable amount of money. However, if you really want to save money, eliminate having a vehicle completely and use public transportation. The bus, train, and occasional taxi is always cheaper in the long run. Unfortunately most people need a car in the USA just to get to work, due to the large distances between destinations, and the usual lack of good public transport. Even so, to buy a car that is always giving trouble is a recipe for eventual financial disaster.

Gasoline: Of course, when you are trying to reduce expenditures, you need to be aware of when you use your car and whether the ride you are taking is absolutely necessary, so as to save on gas. Also, a thing to be aware of is that there is a significant amount of gasoline used in a motor vehicle upon starting it. This is due in part to the vehicle's cold engine, when the moving parts have a greater resistance. Because of this, driving small distances is always less efficient with gasoline than longer distances. Also, driving somewhere in a hurry can hurt gas mileage significantly. The type of thing that I have seen is that drivers, starting up after a red light, put their foot to the floor to speed up, notwithstanding that they can see another red light ahead. I have noticed that the same people will accelerate into a stop sign, screeching to a stop, and hurting the economy of the car while also causing the brake pads to wear out significantly. Driving like this can cause poor mileage, often by a factor of 40%—meaning that for every ten gallons in the tank, four are totally wasted. To save money, learn to drive in a smooth and steady manner. For short distances, learn to walk.

Vacations: Vacations are great, but they have to be budgeted for. If you are having hard times, then postpone an expensive vacation until you can afford it. Rather, take vacations that are local, easy, and have little or no cost. Camping and outdoor hikes in wilderness parks come to mind as being healthy, fun and relatively inexpensive. Short holidays can be very relaxing, but not if you have to worry about the payment.

Home upkeep, repairs, and renewals: Home upkeep is essential. To have a nice home and not keep it in good condition is a short-sighted way to save money. So how do you keep it in good condition? Well, if you don't know how to fix something in the home, then learn how! Sure, it will take you two or three times as long, but once you have done it, even if you make mistakes and it does not look quite like a professional job, you will never be afraid of doing it again. Buying a do-it-yourself book can pay high dividends. Not only do you save money, but you also learn valuable skills. Paying for help when you have the time and could have done it yourself is a luxury you might not be able to afford.

What to do if you already have debt

There are some debts that you may be able to lessen or minimize, especially when you are at the end of your rope and feel that there is no escape but bankruptcy.

Hospital bills: If you have medical bills that have escalated and you want to pay them but do not have the money to do so, what can you do? You have another option other than to declare bankruptcy, and that is to offer to pay 50% of the bill outright, if you can raise or get the funds from another source. It is interesting that the medical fraternity will not normally take their creditors to court; such action is very much the exception. They give their overdue accounts to a debt collector, who is always ready to negotiate a smaller payment to clear the account, or at least willing to make some sort of arrangement.

I once had a medical bill that I thought was way too much for what was done. I offered to pay 50%, and the medical facility refused and said it was their policy not to negotiate. Later I had a call from a debt collector. I told them that I had previously offered to pay 50% because of my complaint and was still prepared to pay 50%. Immediately they responded by asking me to send them a check for that amount and that the debt would be cleared. I wrote on the left (bottom) hand side of the check "*In full and final settlement of the account.*" This is a very important thing to write on such checks. If it is cashed, you will legally be out of harm's way. I sent it off and never heard another word from anyone!

While owing money might be painful in several ways, I have yet to see companies take their individual debtors to court for the recovery of sums under $10,000. This is due to two or three factors. First, the cost of suing an individual for any sum is high. Secondly, what is the good of creditors' suing if the debtor has no assets? I have found that professional people and institutions, such as doctors and hospitals, only rarely go after the people that they have done business with. It would give them a bad image to other would-be customers, don't you see?

If you find yourself in such a situation, try to negotiate a smaller amount. Almost certainly you will be able to reduce the bill by 50%. And if push comes to shove and you just do not have the money, then delay the payments or make very small ones. Where medical bills are concerned, there are often extenuating circumstances, and a good deal of sympathy for the responsible party, such as the head of family who has to pay for the emergency treatment of children or spouses.

Credit Card Debt: How many credit cards or offers of credit have you received in the past year? One? Five? Ten? How about two per month? It seems that almost everyone in the so-called western world has or uses credit cards. Banks and credit card issuers are always touting better deals. Credit cards are an almost (but not quite) essential item for anyone who buys, rents, or travels. The problem with credit cards is that they are difficult to manage responsibly. With credit cards we are able to buy whatever we want or see, whether we can afford it or not. In this way it's a great temptation to misuse them, and then very soon we have an expensive debt hanging over our heads.

The only good way to use credit cards is to pay the full outstanding amount at the end of each month. By using credit cards in this way you will establish a clean and enviable credit score. The disaster approach is to run your card up to its limit on a continuing basis, just paying the minimum amount due, which includes part of all past fees and interest charges that in effect are compounded each month. The minimum due is generally 5% of the total owing, which means that if the outstanding balance were $3,000, 5% would be $150. This amount would pay off very little of the principle debt, if any. The minimum payment always goes first to pay off all of the interest, fees, and late charges. If there's anything left over it will go to the principle. The accumulated interest, fees, and late charges would be a sizable portion of that $150, maybe half.

If you always pay only the minimum on your bills, life will become stressful and your future will be uncertain, partly because of the excessive interest charges that you will incur, and partly because you will be unable to put away money for later investments that you will need to make if you wish for a better financial future. In time this may make it difficult for you to afford the necessities of everyday living. Cars, holidays, clothing, and even other household necessities become luxuries you simply cannot afford. The possibility of having to rent accommodation for the rest of your life becomes real, as you cannot afford the down payment on a house, or have the credit rating necessary for a mortgage.

The interest charges on credit cards do not seem much unless you look at the percentage on a yearly basis. The true percentage ranges around 24% per year. An APR (Annual Percentage Rate) of 24% would mean that for each dollar that you do not pay monthly, you have to pay 24 cents extra, or nearly one quarter of what you owe, each year. Put another way, if there is an item that you just have to buy because it is a bargain or on sale, it would not look such a good buy if you had to pay another quarter of the price over and above what you did in fact pay for it. The bargains that you see are only a bargain if you don't have to pay hidden costs.

With credit cards or any debt you may have, you need only work it out for yourself. By paying only the minimum amount, it will be, in most cases, impossible to pay off your balance entirely or ever to get out of debt permanently unless there is a determined effort to change your spending habits. For each $1,000 of debt, the likelihood of having to pay finance charges of $240 each year means that in a five-year period, you would pay an additional amount of $1,200, over and above the base debt of $1,000. Every five years, you would pay your debt more than twice over. If periodic late charges were added, such as late fees six time a year, then the total cost over 5 years could mount up to another $1,000! All money that is, in effect, wasted.

It is easy to see that fixed debts are like carrying around a permanent ball and chain. A debt of $1,000 will, in effect, cost you $1,000 to $2,000 every five years. And for what? Those few expenditures that you thought that you would like to purchase? Most probably you cannot even remember where you spent the money and for what. Certainly you wished you had not. Now it feels too late. But it is never too late! Certainly it takes quite a bit of resolve to change or adjust a lifetime habit of spending. It will depend on the amount of pain you have already had. Starting to take charge is always the first step and is never too late to do.

Who is in charge of your financial future? You are! You must get out from being a slave to a credit! Eventually, if you cannot pay it off, you may need to seek help to get your affairs in order.

It turns out that credit card companies always have huge, hard to collect amounts owed. Because of this, they are often quite amenable to getting some of their debt paid off rather than none at all. It costs them a lot of money to deal with delinquencies, so they will sometimes look at a suggestion to pay less over a longer period, even to the extent of freezing the principle balance, meaning you can no longer use your card. They are often willing to take a reduced payment to clear the principle balance, even half the amount, more especially if you can get someone to pay the amount immediately in cash. Sometimes they will be willing to forgive some of their charges if they can see it is in their best interest. But do not expect that you can start up another card. Your credit will be shot for some years to come because of your record. You will have a bad credit rating and will become known for that by the other various lending institutions.

Finally, do not be sucked into enticements by those who promise you a credit card even with your bad credit rating. They are in the business of taking your money. They will give you a low limit on a card and charge you a hefty annual fee. Interest will be high. The grace period will be shorter, so that you will almost have to pay the day after you receive their bill. Such people have innovative ways of getting your money. Don't be fooled.

More money is not the answer

I have a relative who, many years ago, just could not manage his money. He always needed more, and often would get himself into trouble because he failed to control his expenses. He would look at his income and decide what he could spend it on. When additional expenses turned up that he had not allowed for or had forgotten to take into account, he was unable to pay them, so he borrowed in order to ease the problem, not realizing that he had in fact just added to his financial woes.

One of the times that I saw him, I said, "Why do you not have a monthly budget that will keep you out of the various problems that you constantly have?" He said to me, "I do not need a budget. I need money!" Needless to say, I have laughed every time I recall what he said. Money was not the answer to his problems. The solution always lies in what is done with the money you get. That is the difference between financial success and financial failure.

It is important to recognize that money cannot make a person happy. Both those who are rich and those who are poor can be unhappy, regardless of how much money they have. Having money can even be a curse if there is no plan to wisely use it.

The stories of people coming into unexpected money and being worse off for it are legendary. In fact, there are several counseling organizations for those who win the lotteries and who find that they are not happy about all the new friends they have suddenly acquired. Many of these people find that, rather than a blessing, their "good fortune" ruined not only their lives but also the lives of their family. Some were able, with good counseling, to survive such a windfall. Others were less fortunate.

I remember there were two people who won the English Football Pools many years ago. The first was a man who, being a careful spender, always purchased retread tires for his car. When he won this large amount, he immediately went and purchased a nearly new Jaguar. He decided that he would buy a new set of tires for the car, but insisted that they were retread tires in order to avoid paying the full price of the new ones. He then drove it up the A1 highway, north of London, where he knew that he could really see what the Jaguar could do. In those days tires were not as long lasting or as safe as they are today. He found out too late that retread tires are not good to drive at high speeds. The treads separated while he was speeding and the Jaguar flipped over. He died in the accident.

The second person won a huge amount of money, the equivalent of well over five million dollars. He had worked as a mechanic in a metal working shop. He immediately gave up his job and decided to buy a home in the country and live it up by giving parties and inviting his old friends and new acquaintances. Many evenings each month he had these parties, where it seemed there were more and more "friends." He hired a servant to manage his household affairs, as well as staff to take care of the cleaning and cooking. He had read how it was to live in style and had decided to do so. He also purchased sev-eral cars, with a chauffeur to drive him to various places of enter-tainment. His health deteriorated. He put on weight, and became an alcoholic. He found that he could not sleep well unless he had alcohol in his system. He got up later and later each day.

Finally after several years, having arranged with an accountant to pay all of the bills that came in, his accountant said that there was no money left. He was effectively cleaned out. There were no more parties for pleasure and no more friends to give him comfort. The home and cars had to be sold, and his staff left.

In the end he had to find a job working for a lesser wage than he originally had, using his wages to pay for a one-room apartment and his food. Oh, how he bitterly regretted wasting all the money he had won! It was reported that he wished heartily that he had never won the money in the first place because he ended up so much worse off than before.

The importance of not spending more than you earn

In the mid 1800s, the author Charles Dickens, in *David Copperfield*, wrote about a character named Micawber. This character seemed always to be in financial trouble. In this story, Micawber remarks, "Annual income twenty pounds, annual expenditure nineteen pounds nineteen and six, result happiness. Annual income twenty pounds, annual expenditure twenty pounds and six, result misery." (The amounts quoted are £20.00, £19.975 and £20.025, in the United Kingdom's present, decimal, currency.) What Micawber was saying was that when anyone regularly spends less than is received, their future will be bright, but when anyone regularly spends more than is received, even just a little bit more, the result spells a future of misery.

Unfortunately, many people live from paycheck to paycheck and never seem to be able to get out of the habit of spending more than they earn, hence the cash checking businesses that will instantly cash post-dated and out-of-state checks for a hefty fee, and are pleased to lend money against the title of people's cars at enormous interest. The borrowers think, "If only I had some more money!" Meanwhile, they are giving away their money to the moneylenders.

Again, more money is rarely the answer; what we do with the money we have is the important thing. It is indeed sad that people don't realize this.

If you think that having money is the solution, I can tell you that I have known people who are considered financially rich, yet they are in the same financial mess as those who have one tenth of their income.

I once rented a house to one such family. Their income was in the region of $250,000 each year or so they said. They had five children. On the outside, people thought this family was well off; they had a very nice, well-kept, high-end home—a home they rented from me—in a good neighborhood. Everyone could see their three new cars and SUVs in the driveway and a motor cruiser that could be towed to the local lake on weekends. The children's friends enjoyed playing the various video games that were in abundance in the basement. All seemed ideal with them to every outward appearance.

The reality was quite different. They wanted to be thought of as well-off, so they spent a great deal of time—and money—showing others just how rich they were. In reality, each of the vehicles was being leased, as was the boat. Their credit cards were close to their limits on a continuing basis. Unfortunately, they also felt that they had to indulge their children by buying them the latest gadgets to show off to their friends; they would buy whatever their children wanted, thus spoiling them and sowing the seeds of discontent for their children later in life. They kept trying to find ways to get extra money, which they thought would cure all of their financial problems.

Eventually I learned that on a previous home, not only did they have a first mortgage, but a second mortgage as well. They had to file for bankruptcy so as to protect themselves from their creditors and to keep living in their home for a time at least. Later, after they moved out of my home, I learned that their motor vehicles, boat, and trailer had been repossessed. They learned a hard lesson and started to climb out of the financial hole that they had dug for themselves. Furthermore, because they had so much debt, they could not get credit from any bank or lending institution. Their credit cards were made inactive so that they had to live on a cash basis, paying their bills with just the money that they had coming in.

On the other side I know of a family who were on minimum income, close to the official poverty level but were able to support a small mortgage on a small home. This family was responsible with money, and brought up seven loving children who learned to work in the vegetable garden and do household repairs. Later, those children worked their way through college and became responsible adults, with a healthy respect for what money could and could not do. Boy, did those children appreciate the value of money, preparing them well for their own future financial success.

I do not know if the family who took out bankruptcy requested help from friends or relations. Anyone lending them money beyond a certain amount would have done them a disservice because only some level of pain to them could cure such gross mismanagement. To take that pain away from them would have sown the seeds for a later relapse into their old habits. Where financial matters are concerned, some sort of pain always seems necessary.

It is easy to see how important it is to be able to manage your income, no matter what level of income you have. A penny saved is a penny earned, so it is said, and I do believe it to be true. Sure, to be self-sufficient, it may mean you must live in a very small home, trailer or apartment, or grow some of your own food, which is widely practiced in Eastern Europe and many other parts of the world. But it is worth the effort in order to become financially secure and to start being able to plan for the future. It is never too late to start. Never!

What to do if you gain a lot of money quickly

So what happens if you do happen to gain a large amount of money quickly?

Actually, most of us, young and old in the Western World and in many other countries, will become owners of a substantial amount of money in our lifetime that we have not worked for. The question is, what should we do with it when it comes? Now is the time to plan what we would do, before it happens. Will we be ready and know how to handle the money or its equivalent?

A windfall can come in many ways: the amount may be an inheritance, or payout from insurance (either a policy or damages to us), a retirement payout or annuity, or the sale of a property or bus-iness, etc. It is extremely important that such money is not allowed to dissipate through bad practices. I guarantee that if you have an unexpected influx of money at any time in your life, there will be an almost irresistible urge to waste it on things that, with good thinking, you would not otherwise do.

Looking to your future needs is of the utmost importance. This will of course depend on your age and circumstances. Most of us will be in our middle life when it happens but it can happen at any time, so I will start with the very young, where there is some guardianship situation or other entity to take care of the money.

A Windfall while Young: First, if money is left to the young, the welfare of the young is of first importance and the preservation of the capital being a number one priority. It is very important to have the principle sum safeguarded, while adjusting it for inflation.

In trying to do this, to put the assets into a fixed-income mode like savings would be the worst thing to do. This is because the young person or persons would then see the value of their assets dissipate over time through inflation, fees, charges and other expenses.

If the money were used to bring temporary assistance, this would be wrong too. What is needed is to use the money in such a way that the receiver will have benefits for life—in other words, to take the person

55

to a higher level of financial security. In order to do this, investment in the stock market as outlined in the chapter on long-term investing would be probably the best option. The purchasing of rental property would be another.

Young adults, such as teenagers through age 21, who have large amounts of money come to them, need help to handle it. If they have immediate control of the money, they would need a considerable amount of discipline, which is seldom possible at that age. The sudden new wealth opens up all types of supposedly good opportunities; however, the correct procedure would be for them to sit down and think of their future and what they would like to do with their lives. Investing the new wealth in such a way as to get a continuing income while also preserving the principle would be best. It would need to be inflation-proof. This can be done, again, by way of the stock market as explained in the long-term investing chapter.

It's not too bad to let young people learn about money the hard way while they are still young, but they should not be allowed to use the whole of the money—perhaps 10% of the principle should be enough for them to learn how easy it is to squander it. However, it is also good practice for them to exercise their minds and consequentially think things through; that will teach them valuable lessons. After all, it is not necessary to put one's hand on a red hot stove to find out that it is an unwise decision.

A Windfall in Mid-life: While less likely to take the irresponsible path, those who come into some level of increased wealth, especially during their mid-life period, tend to breathe a sigh of relief and decide to pay off their mortgage, have a long wished for vacation, and otherwise spend a good portion of it. Any residue might be banked for a rainy day. This too is wasteful and is invariably regretted at a later date. By all means ease up on the level of hardship, if it is present, but why take action that will put you back into that hardship mode in the future? That is not a sensible approach. Consequences need to be thought through thoroughly now. No, the best plan would be to use no more than one-sixth of the money to lessen the hardship that is present now and then use the remainder to create a better future.

Depending on the amount of the windfall, paying off a long-term fixed rate mortgage is usually a low priority. I elsewhere stress the advantages of a mortgage because of the benefits due to inflation and tax deductions, provided that in the early years the monthly payments are easily covered within a disciplined budget. However, if the amount of money is so large as to be able to clear all debts and also leave a long-term, inflation-proof income, then by all means do so. The most important thing is to create that long-term, inflation-proof income.

It would be best to put most of the available funds into some investment that will appreciate over the long term, such as is outlined in the long-term investing chapter. Another such investment might be some land that could be held over an extended period of time, like twenty to thirty years. You could then sell it, little by little, according to your needs. With this approach, property taxes and other expenses would have to be budgeted for from another income.

Another way the money could be used would be to buy some income-producing property such as an apartment block or business premise and then get a rental agency to handle the issue of actually renting out the property and dealing with maintenance and other costs. It is reasonable to assume that you would get better than 8% return on investment after all expenses. This method is good because it brings in some income, and also the property appreciates in value in line with inflation. Know, however, that absentee landlords are notoriously at risk, so it is important in this type of investment to have a good rental agent. A good rental agent is worth his weight in gold and every penny of his fees, usually 7% to 9% of the amount of rent he collects. This will depend on the amount of work involved and how many properties you have your agent managing. If you get one for less than that, they may not do a decent job.

I do not recommend buying an actual business under the circumstance of receiving a large amount of money. If you have not already entered a business by the time that you are at midlife, then your chances of success are greatly lessened. You lack experience. Businesses are notoriously fickle, often surviving no more than ten years, the reasons for this being many and varied, as explained later in this book (see Chapter Five on starting a business).

A Windfall Later in Life: What happens if the large windfall is received even later in life? If you have lived most of your life in a fairly comfortable position, but require income for your later years, the sudden delivery of a nice nest egg can blind the mind from seeing consequences. The "safest" investment, you think, is to put it all, or most of it, into a savings or interest-bearing account with a view to living off the interest for the rest of your life. This would not be a wise thing to do. If you knew the actual date of your demise it would be different, but a supposedly safe savings account is only safe for a few years. I have seen so many people put their money in this type of "safe" investment only to find out later that the value of their funds has diminished due to inflation to the point that they don't have enough to live on, at least in the manner to which they have become accustomed. This type of thing occurs most often with people who retire with a fixed pension or lump sum payment, thinking that they will be able to live a comfortable life until they pass on. If they would think it through, they would realize that in this day and age, with steadily increasing prices for goods and services, accompanied with some level of inflation, their expectations are doomed to failure.

Conclusion

Budgeting is the first and primary key in gaining control of your personal finances. You know how much you bring in each month, or each pay period, but do you really know what you spend? Until you do, you are not truly in control of your money—rather, it is in control of you!

We all want to make more money, but having a larger income is rarely the answer. Exercising a little self-discipline, making wise financial decisions, and working to pay off and stay out of debt is far more beneficial in the long term than simply seeking ways to make more money—especially if you simply spend it.

Sudden wealth typically proves more of a pitfall than a windfall when one has not learned to use wisely the money one already has. I have seen many people in my lifetime become rich suddenly, only to find that their unwise use of that money creates disastrous consequences, especially when they receive something suddenly like a prize or the lottery. Luckily, as mentioned before, there are associations for people who have come into sudden wealth. They often suggest geting the immediate assistance of a lawyer and eventually a financial planner and/or CPA. These professionals help you not make decisions too fast. The saying goes, act in haste, repent at leisure! Yes, I too have had my share of repenting at leisure, it cannot be avoided in life, but we can minimize the repetition of it. To do the right thing with money may take some re-evaluation of the broad picture, but doing it right pays handsome dividends.

CHAPTER THREE

Scams: What They Are and How They Work

Most of us have come across a scam in one form or another, even if we were unaware of it at the time. A scam is a condition set up by an enterprising person (or persons) commonly called a con artist or confidence trickster, who wants the victim to give them something— usually money. They want to take from the victim, but do not want to steal from them. Rather than committing an outright crime, scammers want their victims to give up their goods willingly and with- out any fuss.

These people work on the premise that it is a legitimate enterprise which they are representing, even that the law is on their side, which it often is, unfortunately. The scammers frequently cannot be taken to court because you have willingly given the scammers what they want – at least initially—therefore they have not "robbed" you in the strict interpretation of the word, although they do in fact rob from you… you just don't realize it at the time!

There are thousands of scams going on at any given time. I some- times marvel at the ingenuity of these people who keep inventing new ways to take you in. Scammers operate world-wide and can vary from just one person to the very largest of businesses like Enron or the old World Com.

Though specifics tend to change because of changes in society and technology, principles do not and are generally as valid today as those in Roman times. One of these principles is that human nature is the same today as it has always been. This means con men are as ever- present as they have always been, and that victims and "suckers" are also as available as ever.

When I worked at the British War Office in 1948, I allowed someone to try to scam me just to see where it would lead. I enjoyed every minute of it, because I felt I knew how to protect myself. It was only later that I realized that I was not the main target, but rather background cover for this person's schemes on others.

The story was that I worked in the cipher department decoding intelligence from around the world. Nearby was an Underground station. While I was making a call in the station's telephone box, there was a knock on the window by a gentleman asking to "borrow" a penny to complete his three-penny phone call. After his call, he invited me to have afternoon tea with him.

He presented himself as a larger-than-life personality. He had an I.D. indicating he was a member of the press. He was an assistant manager at a West End movie theater, too. He could and did get me free tickets. Besides this, he had an "in" to London Society that allowed me to attend some interesting gatherings. He cloaked much of his life in secrecy and confided in me that he did intelligence work at the American Embassy.

It all seemed too good to be true—which is usually a good indicator that something is. Also, why would he want to befriend someone like me? In addition, he seemed able to obtain certain goods that were scarce and highly sought after in post-war England, like silk stockings and American chewing gum. Anything of a scarce nature he was able to get. I suspected he was a confidence trickster, but decided that by being friends with him and observing him, I could learn a lot.

Many things didn't add up. Once when I phoned the American Embassy to enquire if he were there, I discovered that he didn't work there at all; he wasn't a newspaper reporter either. From his aunt I discovered that he wasn't an American as he claimed (though he talked with an American accent). Later on I tended to feel sorry for him; he was so enthusiastic and wanted to succeed. If only he had put his talents into a worthwhile career he would have gone far.

The Scammer

Scammers come in all shapes and sizes. There are individual scammers, scammers who work as a group, and now, in today's world, companies and corporations whose main function is to obtain money from the unwary consumer. They all use situations to get you to do something that under normal circumstances you would not do. Once they recognize that you have something that they want, be it money, goods, or property, they will pursue you in order to relieve you of the burden of ownership.

You might think that only people without substance or money perpetrate scams. This is not true. Some are successful enough in their earlier years through their charms and drive that they rise up, often in the corporate field, and gain promotions within businesses, to the extent that they are able to practice their art at a very high level. Often they are found out only after having done much mischief and causing pain and heartache to many. Don't think that high executives cannot be scammers—many can be, as evidenced in early 2000 when fraudulent behaviors were discovered in the commodities and stock market, in the way of gold and land frauds.

Some people think of scammers as romantic creatures, especially when they are portrayed in books or movies. In reality they are robbers: they steal from anyone they can, without the slightest feeling of remorse. The better ones make a full-time living at it. Others are merely in it for the game—it's a challenge and a skill to them. The victim can be rich, poor, young or old; it makes no difference.

So, knowing that confidence tricksters exist in the world, what are their character traits? Here are some of them:

- They are very good at assessing human nature and manipulating it.
- They are good at deducing what it will take to entice other humans to part with their money, land or goods.
- They love what they do. They get a high from it!
- They think that they are smarter than others. They believe they can take something from less-intelligent people quite easily.

- They keep away from those that they assess as being like themselves. They also keep away from those who have had prior experience with scammers.
- They are often convincing because they believe their own scam. They don't see themselves as bad. They rationalize what they are doing, and they are good at projecting their need as more important than any sense of compassion. This character trait can make them very believable, and therefore very successful.
- They want something you have. Scammers are always geared to your ability to pay (sometimes to pay several times). They will keep at it until you are left with little or nothing left for them to go after.
- They are good actors. Scammers at the intermediate level will often portray themselves as respectable and successful. They are adept at putting on a suitable front to impress others.
- They explore new and devious ways to practice their art. They are constantly thinking of ways to make better and more effective scams at the expense, of course, of their victims.

The next step here is how do we identify a potential scammer? They have several identifying traits:
- They seem to be nice and friendly. It is easy to like them. This is part of their stock-in-trade.
- They promise the world. Be wary of those who will promise you virtually any level of riches for your investment. They appeal to your greed and then trip you up with it.
- They make you feel guilty if you do not follow them. If you foil them, you are the bad guy!

Scams

Scams change with time to suit the particular circumstances. In the Middle Ages, the scams might have centered around land, position, or money. Examples of such a scam might be the turning of lead into gold; or perhaps the extension of life by selling some worthless or even dangerous potion, such as mercury (given to some Mongol chiefs, as recounted by Marco Polo). A woman who married ten times only to kill each of her husbands for his money was also a type of scammer, using her artfulness to achieve her aims.

I am sure the list was long back then and is probably longer now because we have more prosperity and more advancements in society, such as electronic equipment, home improvements, and various types of financial instruments. The result is that today the average scammer has more fuel for his talents.

My first acquaintance with a scam was about sixty-five years ago. I was eleven years old and I had been evacuated out of London to avoid the bombing that was taking place. I was moved to Carmarthen, South Wales, for the duration of the Second World War. I was on my own and could not ask anyone for advice. I was not a naturally outgoing boy, rather self-contained in fact. Not that I did not like others—but to be part of a group or gang was not my thing.

A boy with whom I had been somewhat acquainted approached me and proposed we be friends. This was unusual, but since I wanted the company, I readily agreed. After a week or so, he proposed we meet on the following Saturday in town to look around and have some fun. Upon meeting the following Saturday, he suggested we go to the movies. I agreed, and he quickly followed up with a request: Could I lend him two shillings? Two shillings was the equivalent of a month's pocket money at the time, and my mother had recently sent me two shillings. He continued: "I really need the money urgently to buy a small present for my foster mother. I will give you back two and sixpence on Monday!"

This sounded a worthy reason for me to lend him the money. His offering to give me sixpence more if I lent him the money would mean that I would get, in effect, an extra week's pocket money. Oh, all the things I could do with the extra sixpence! I said to him, "How can I be sure to get the money back?"

"If I cannot bring it on Monday, then later in the week for sure!" he said. "But I will definitely give it back to you on Monday."

"How can you be sure?" I said again.

"Didn't I tell you?" he said. "I live in a bank!"

We were in the city center and he straightaway took me to where he lived and showed me an apartment above a bank. He said that was where he lived and that his foster parent was the bank manager. How could I resist, if he lived at the bank? I was sure to get my money! At the time it never occurred to me to ask why, if he lived in the bank, he needed to borrow money. Instead I thought that anyone who actually lived in a bank, as opposed to working in it, was bound to have access to money. So I thought, "Here is a way of getting another six pence back, 25% profit, for lending this money to my new friend, and only for two days! He lives at the bank, so it is a sure thing!" I knew the expression, "safe as a bank", so I gave him the money.

Needless to say, I never saw that two shillings again. On the next day he avoided me, and from that day on if I was able to talk to him, which was not often, he would make some excuse or promise that was never fulfilled. So I lost a doubtful friend and my two shillings, which represented four weeks of my pocket money. Am I sorry it happened? Goodness no, for it taught me a great lesson of not putting much credence in unsubstantial or misleading words, more especially when something was required of me, either money, goods, or effort. The other lesson I learned, which is also a truism, is that one way to lose a friend is to lend them money. I lost my money and my newfound friend, although I later suspected that he had only become my friend so that he could scrounge some money off me.

Have I ever been taken since? Never like the first time. Now I only go along with a scam when I am interested in seeing how it is to be worked, but I never go to the point where they take my money or goods. So next time you get that wonderful opportunity or are asked to lend an acquaintance some money (be especially careful of relations) watch out! Only give or lend money that you will not need. Then you can hope—but do not expect—to get it back. That way you will keep them as friends.

Identifying a scam

So how do you identify a scam so that you can steer clear of it? The chances of you getting scammed or otherwise being on the wrong side of a financial opportunity in your lifetime are extremely high. The following will hopefully minimize these stressful situations by showing you how to avoid them. First, avoid those who by the previous list you can identify as a scammer. But secondly, beware of the scams that come your way that fulfill the following characteristics. Spotting a scam is relatively easy, if you know what to look for.

- *It is the opportunity of a lifetime!* The more a proposal is extraordinary, the more likely that it will turn out to be a scam, and thus should be avoided—the sooner the better. It makes no difference where or from whom the great opportunity comes: a well-known personality, company, a remote relation, or just a friend of a friend. Confidence tricksters are not called such for nothing...they trick your confidence!
- *It is an ongoing permanent opportunity!* You are led to believe that your financial future will be much enhanced with the steady addition of wealth or income.
- *There is no risk involved!* The presentation seems to be risk-free, and it seems you cannot be the loser or be poorer off.
- *It's an easy proposition requiring you to do little for a large return!* It is like taking candy from a baby! This is often the approach when scammers use a large entity as their cover, such as government or a large business, in order to impress you with the validity of their proposal.
- *You are smarter than the others involved!* The scammer portrays himself as a lucky person who has somehow stumbled onto some opportunity. He wants you to think that you too can have inside knowledge and should take advantage of this unique situation. Beware of such portrayals! If you think that you have the upper hand in any proposal, you may well be in danger if you proceed!
- *It's a secret!* If there is a proposal that you "must not talk about" to others because if you do the "new opportunity" would go away, be very careful, because that is a red flag.

- *You can make a killing!* This is a direct appeal to your greed. Perhaps you have been wanting more money in order to do certain things with your life. Now comes this special opportunity to get into the big time, a kind of out-of-the-blue financial catapult to success. You think, "Look at what I could do with all that money!" Don't be so dazzled by the prospect that you succumb, because this appeal to your greed for more money is likely a scam. The scammer's job and expertise always relies on the victim's greed level...that is, the victim's wish to benefit beyond his or her normal expectations.
- *If you do not take this opportunity, someone else will!* Scammers make you feel this way to get you to act quickly, without thinking things through. Beware of those who make you feel the opportunity will be lost if you do not act right away.

As an illustration, let us take an example of two nice older sisters whom you might meet at a social event. After infiltrating your confidence, they might suggest a course of action that they think will benefit you financially, though it may not be a large sum in relative terms. It may be just to let you know that they are somewhat in poor financial circumstances and that they are proud siblings trying to get by. They are willing to dispose of some of their heirlooms that were left to them by their great-grandfather who lived 150 years ago; something that they have always treasured. There is an odd hint that there is a picture that was painted by some famous artist. They let slip a name that you recognize as an old master—yet they do not show any understanding of the name like you do. They would love to sell this item, whatever it is, at a price that would be far below what you think that it could be worth, even though it still represents a fair sum of money to you. You have been hooked and are being gently reeled in!

It is suggested that you might like to buy the painting or other article of worth. Your greed takes over and you think you could buy this article for a sum that would be only a fraction of its real worth. So you part with your money, acquire the painting, and then they disappear—happy that their scam was again successful. Eventually you find that you had paid a lot of money for a fake. By the time you find out that you have been scammed, they cannot be located. You are embarrassed to find out that you have been had!

What are the traits from the previous list that would help you identify this as a scam? There is the mystery element present. There is the greed on your part to make a killing. You think there is the wealth to you without any risk. You think you have the upper hand. You just know that if you do not take this opportunity, someone else will. You are of course smarter than they are. It's an easy proposition requiring you to do little for a large return. While it may not be an opportunity of a lifetime, it is still very good for you.

How can you avoid this from happening to you? The answer is to study and be aware of the signs of a scam. The more that you like the deal the more wary you should become. Do not ever regret missing a lost opportunity. The real thing will come along in due time. There are so many people who want something for nothing, meaning they want your something for their nothing! You need not be ashamed of missing an "extra good" deal, it is most usually not the extra good deal you thought it was.

The ingredients for a scam are many and varied; however when you are offered something that looks great, wait while you think through the reasons why you are being offered such an opportunity. What is in it for the other person or organization? Is it a "special deal"? Such inside special deals need to be looked at very carefully. You need to ask yourself, "Why me? What is so special about me that I should be offered a 'special deal'?" I can say, after a lifetime of being offered special deals, I have found very often the giver of the "special deal" is far better off for giving it than you are for receiving it!

I was present in a location in Utah where a scam took place that illustrates well the elements contained within a successful scam. A particular person moved into our local community and church. In a subtle way we, the members of our community, soon learned what type of business he was in, something where we could get a 3% dividend on our investment—EACH MONTH! Supposedly without the slightest risk!

He was a representative of an off-shore business enterprise that dealt in commodities on a world-wide basis, twenty-four hours a day. The investment was "guaranteed to succeed" because no commodity was purchased before there was a buyer somewhere in the world willing to purchase the commodity at a higher price, even at only a few cents higher. They matched up both buyer and seller so that there was a profit.

We were told that because the quantity bought and sold at any one time was very large, the relative amount of profit was considerable. This company and the person representing the organization were soliciting more investment so that more capital could be used for its operation and thereby produce more profits. It was represented that there could not be a loss on any transaction as all trades were virtually instantaneous. Some local residents attended the seminar and decided to invest a moderate amount to try it out. After all, they said, it is a far better return than anything else that was available, like bank CD's etc.

At the end of the first three months the people who became involved found that they had already received nine percent on their original investment. Because of this some decided to put more money into the scheme. By the ninth month there was a positive flood of people putting money into the scheme. Some even mortgaged their homes to increase their investment.

After the first fifteen months had gone by the monthly checks started being delayed and then finally stopped coming. The gentleman who had been soliciting for the business told everyone who had a complaint that he was upset at the way his employers had let him down, and then he moved out of our community! I am not sure, but I suspect that he might have been as much a victim as the investors. He had been recruited and trained to believe what he had been told. It was likely that he was taken in with the scheme so as to be able to convince others of its validity. He told me that he was paid a fixed salary and commissions—based upon his performance no doubt!

It was a well thought out and executed scheme. Yet you will notice that it had all of the ingredients for a scam. Quick and easy money from what at first looked like a very reasonable and legitimate business model. No risk. The opportunity of a lifetime! You may ask if I participated. No I did not. Yet I had no hard evidence to advise others not to participate. The thing that I did not like was the absence of a US address. It was an off-shore address in the Bahamas because, it was said, the taxes on profits would be too excessive and would significantly reduce the payout to all the hundreds of investors. Yet, being outside the jurisdiction of the US made the possibility of getting justice at a later date within the US very remote.

I came across another scam while I was in the British Army, stationed in Singapore in 1951. I had several very good friends at the time who always enjoyed my ability to make a special brew of iced tea. We would often talk about things we wanted to do when we were back in England; getting a job, starting a business, etc. On one occasion I arrived at my friends' place to find that there was a local "entrepreneur" who had a proposal for starting a new business venture in Singapore. He claimed he had found a good location, just outside one of the army camps, where business would be great.

It was for a British fish-and-chip shop. He said that he had the site and could get the staff and all of the equipment, yet lacked the capital to complete the project. While giving his proposal he said that he had already got some other army personnel to agree to invest and would we like to get in on the ground floor of this new project? He explained that he had worked out that there was a fortune to be made in such a venture. The initial investment could be returned within six months of opening, and thereafter every six months for an indefinite period. My friends said what a wonderful opportunity it was and would I like to invest also? The entrepreneur looked pleasing and encouraging; he was a good, persuasive talker.

I said that he should phone us in two days' time, that perhaps we could get others to participate too. He said that with more investment, it would be possible to open several more shops and make even more money. Would we like to make a down payment now to solidify our willingness to invest—say $500? I said, no, that we would see what could be done within these next two days, and we would speak to him again after that time.

In the meantime, I had indicated privately to my friends that they should be led by what I said and not to go further. Then later in private, I explained that what we had been told had the ingredients for a classic scam: he promised great gain for an indefinite future, with many benefits to investors, including free fish and chips at any time; here was a golden opportunity to get in on the ground floor of a new and great success story, with future expansions throughout Southeast Asia; now was the time to invest—right now! "Give me your money and you will become very rich," was this fellow's mantra (the classic sprat to catch a mackerel).

On the other hand, nothing was in place for the proposed new business: he had no business plan to show, only promises; there was no specific location for the business; he had no names to give as to the other interested parties; he had no breakdown of actual or anticipated costs; he did not even have anyone who had experience at running a fish-and-chip shop or who had ever worked in one!

There were also several red flags when it came to the "businessman" himself: he wanted a good-faith deposit paid to him personally; he had no money of his own to invest, only his expertise; there was no business name registered, no third party accountant, bank or professional person he could name; he was a one-man band with a good idea but with no substance; finally, he had no track record of previous successes.

I could smell the scam so strongly that I just had to give a good talking to my friends, who had been ready to invest in this "golden opportunity". I heard later that he had obtained several investments from some other army people and then went missing with it. There was no address or phone number where he could be contacted.

In another situation, a friend of mine built up a successful small business. He was smart and eventually decided to sell it to someone. Several years after the sale, these new purchasers were approached to sell their business for a much higher price to what they thought was a large company that was managing many such businesses in the Western United States. This very substantial business offered more than the then going price for such businesses, thereby enticing the owners to sell the business at a large profit (the appeal to greed). There were two requirements, however, and those were that the business had to be free and clear of debt, and that part of the sales price had to be in the form of a promissory note with a good interest rate—issued by this substantial business.

The owners of the business obtained a personal loan to pay off the debts on the business, then allowed the new purchasers to issue an unsecured note (meaning a note with no security pledged behind it if it should fail) to complete the sale, thus allowing the new purchasers who now owned the property outright to pledge the freed assets on the property for a substantial bank loan!

Needless to say, later the new purchasers skimmed the money from their various businesses by keeping the money that was banked from sales and at the same time not paying the various bills for goods that had been delivered. They walked away with several million dollars, leaving all of the note holders of the many small businesses with not only nothing, but debts of their own. The whole scam left many good families having to file for bankruptcy. A whole lifetime of asset building had been wiped out virtually overnight by a well-thought-out and well-executed scam.

Many years ago when I emigrated to Tasmania, the island state of Australia, the preferred way to travel was by ship. I happen to enjoy playing cards and know many types of games. Soon after boarding the month-long cruise from London to Melbourne, Australia, I met two nice, elderly women who indicated that they enjoyed playing a small game of penny poker and would I care to join them and others to have a relaxed morning's play?

I had played poker in the British Army some years earlier, so I felt confident that I could hold my own without losing too much. It was just a penny game, so I thought that the most I could lose would be perhaps up to five shillings in the whole game—a small amount, which I was prepared to do.

There were six of us including the two elderly women. The game commenced and I was able to play quite well, and the other players seemed to do all right too, except for the two elderly women. Still, they hardly lost anything because they threw in their hands so often! The play went on for about one hour then one of the elderly women said to us, "The game is a little slow—how about raising the stakes to six pence?"—meaning now the lowest we could bet each time was six pence. I was hesitant, yet the others, who had been winning moderately, agreed.

After another hour, the other elderly lady said that she was getting a little bored and could the stakes be made more lively by raising them to one shilling or even two shillings? By now I had won a little, but felt that I should only play for stakes that I was comfortable with and that were not beyond my limit, so I declined and an onlooker took my place. However, I was interested to see what happened and came back later in the morning and found that the two nice, elderly women were cleaning up. Everyone was losing except them.

They were sitting on opposite sides of the card table and had indicated earlier that they were just acquaintances who liked a game of cards to pass the time in a pleasant manner. However, upon examination of the play from a distance, I could see that neither of the two ladies ever competed against each other. I kept an eye on the playing and noticed that there was some kind of secret communication between the two of them. I did not see the signals that must have passed between the two 'nice', elderly women while I was playing, partly because they were on opposite sides of the table; however as an onlooker it became clear to me that something was not quite right.

They would never bet against each other in an aggressive way except at certain low-stakes. They would never bet if they had poor cards. However, when one of them had a clear advantage they would clean up the table. This was done by both ladies betting against a better hand aggressively until the third person dropped out, at which time one or the other of the old ladies would abruptly stop and throw in her cards, not even showing what type of hand she had been bidding on. Sometimes they would both fold their hands and not participate in the hand.

In this way, I saw a pattern of play that I did not much like to see, with the 'nice' elderly women steadily but surely cleaning the others out of sizable amounts of money! Each day when I passed by the card room there they were, having a pleasant game of cards, usually with different players. It was all done very casually and with exclamations of surprise. They always acted as if they were new at the game and just having a run of luck.

Towards the end of the cruise, I accidentally found out these two not-so-nice elderly women actually shared a cabin together. I also found out from another lady who had been on a previous cruise that these not-so-nice elderly women were also there, playing cards on that ship as well! I was told that apparently these ladies regularly went on cruises back and forth from England to Australia.

Except for that first time, I had not played with them. So I felt comfortable sitting down with these elderly women in the buffet restaurant on the day before we were to dock in Melbourne. I asked them how they had enjoyed their cruise and how they had fared with the cards. They looked at each other and one of them said, "You know Gordon, we are so fortunate and lucky at cards that we manage to pay for the cost of our cruises by playing cards and winning! It is quite amazing how lucky we both are."

I thought to myself, *it has nothing to do with luck!* However as they were at least forty years my senior, I was not about to challenge them on their hustling. Here again, I was fortunate to have been able to sense that something was not quite right, avoid getting taken, and learn from the experience.

Scams perpetuated on a mass scale

These days we seem to be inundated with special offers, usually for something that we do not want or need. But these offers are so couched that they appear very appealing and too often persuade us to overspend and put ourselves into more debt. Scams that come through the TV, radio, internet, or other media outlets offer the scammer an advantage not otherwise available. More people are reached at one time through the media, and this makes the scam all the more impactful. So, unsurprisingly, scammers work very hard bringing forth their scams through these outlets. If we are to avoid being taken, we must be aware of these types of scams and avoid them.

A good example of a scam perpetuated on a mass scale is the following advertisement which puts forward a "new health plan" from some entity that does not announce their name, just a toll free 800 number. It is only one example of many of similar types that I have seen:

New Health Plan, 7-day open enrollment with no health questions! $10-$40 Max Pay RX Card. Medical/dental, one low price covers individual or entire family— $89.95 per month (individual).

* All prior conditions accepted! * No limitations on usage!

* All ages accepted! * You cannot be singled out for rate increases or cancellations!

* Pricing will never go up once you are a member!

In a separate box there were more great scam statements as follows:

Get health care that includes: doctor visits, hospital visits, emergency room, urgent care facilities, outpatient testing, medical specialist, home healthcare, physical therapy, medical accidents national networks, dental, vision, chiropractic care, hearing, long-term care, elderly care, 24-hour nurse hotline, air ambulance, and immediate maternity.

Business owners: ask for 'Group Department'.

Call Today! 1800 XXXX. Mon-Fri 8am-6pm Open enrollment offer ends Friday!

I am constantly amazed that these people who dream up such solicitations can find it worthwhile to keep sending such outrageous offers that have no hope of paying up. Shame on them! It is a classic scam case. There is a tremendous play on words and promises that cannot possibly be met, yet which appeal to the gullible and the poor to part them from what little they may have.

It's a case of something being offered that's too good to be true. I could of course go into the nitty-gritty of each claim, but will refrain because, if you are reading this book, you can quite clearly put on your consequential thinking cap and come to the same conclusion as I have: No business can promise to pay out more than it gets in—ever! For a little amount of money they offer you the world (which is not possible in a reputable business). They are quite willing to take your first few months' enrollment fees and your first installment. Then when you start making a claim you will find out that you have gone through a lot of hassle only to see that your money is gone. There is, of course, a waiting period! Or perhaps they will continue to string you along by paying a little on your claims but always less than what you pay them.

I feel sorry for those who may have been suckered into a scam such as this and lost their money. There is no legal recourse and in any case the people who have been suckered in do not now have the money to pursue the scammers.

The saying goes that "there's a sucker born every minute." This means that there are many who can be hoodwinked to pay for or do something that they would not normally do. If you have a fax machine or a computer on-line the chances are that you will get a fairly constant stream of solicitations, many of which might well be scams. They appear to be amazing deals! They can go something like this one that I received:

To: All employees

From: Corporate Travel Department.

Our Corporate Travel Department has asked if you would distribute this memo freely to all employees.

Start planning your vacation now! Take advantage of corporate rates. A 4 day 3 night Bahamas cruise and island stay. All meals included on the ship and 5 Days and 4 nights in Orlando with 2 tickets to the theme park of your choice.

ONLY $199 per person. 1st 50 callers only! Plus port tax.

—————BONUS————

EVERY RESERVATION will receive: 3 days and 2 nights in your choice of Puerto Vallarta, Las Vegas, OR Honolulu, Hawaii.

With ROUNDTRIP AIR FARE INCLUDED!

Sale is limited. So Call Today. Toll Free 1-800-XXX-XXXX

If you have received this in error call toll free, xxx to be removed

Just for the heck of it, I once followed one of these along to the next leg by phoning the operator. She had her line of speech very well-rehearsed. "No," she said, "you have been unlucky and are not within the first 50 to call. However, we have a very special deal for you..." etc, etc.

The end result was that they were not offering anything that was suitable. Dates were when they said, but I would have to pay extra to have it when I wanted. The cruise was for three nights but effectively for two days, due to the fact that two of the days are traveling days. The Island stay was at my expense, and quite expensive. Meals were not included. Also the 5 days and 4 nights in Orlando were quite expensive when all meals had to be paid for. I also would be required to take a tour of a time-share condominium, which used up all of one of the vacation days. The tickets to the theme parks had extra costs by way of taxes and they did not include the Disney Theme Parks. Remember that they did say first 50 callers only! Two people had to book and children were extra.

There were other fees, including booking fees, all of which had to be paid in advance by credit card. Altogether, the advance money amounted to several hundred dollars, and was not refundable. As for the BONUS of another two nights in Puerto Vallarta, Las Vegas or Honolulu Hawaii, space was so limited that the only place left was Las

Vegas, the booking fees were extra and the free airfare was limited to a distant airport, not from where I lived. I could imagine the type of accommodation that might be reserved for my wife and me in Las Vegas...perhaps within five miles of the strip!

Port taxes and the basic cost plus other taxes and fees meant that my costs for a questionable vacation with many unknowns would set me back well over $1000 instead of the advertised $400. And that did not include any children. My head was fairly buzzing after talking to the lady.

You may also notice that the solicitation did not name their organization or address—anything that would help me later to track them down. I would almost certainly have lost the $400 deposit, plus prepaid taxes and fees. Needless to say, I did not proceed. I did not give them any of the money requested as I could not imagine ever seeing it again. So much for the special corporate opportunity! Remember, when something looks too good to be true it generally is.

An e-mail can be sent to thousands of people at a time. If the success rate is just two percent, the perpetrators can make a killing financially. One common email scam runs something like this:

I am a high official in the government of (an African country). There is some surplus money that I have to dispose of. The money, amounting to $26,000,000 (twenty-six million) U.S. dollars needs to be transferred to a bank in the United States. However I am not able to do it myself, because I am a government official and am precluded from legally doing so. The money is surplus and there are no demands on it, it having been the original deposit on a contract that has been fulfilled, leaving the deposit unclaimed.

My associates and I wish to locate an honest person or business associate in order to facilitate the funds' smooth transfer to a US bank that we will name at a later time. This is a private and confidential transaction and we trust that we have found you as an honest person.

For your assistance in enabling the smooth transfer, we are pleased to offer you a 25% commission of the sum in question. Please reply with your acceptance of our offer. We rely on you having a confidential approach to the transaction. Please phone me or fax your answer and we will advise you of the time of such transfer to your own personal account, for further distribution to another account in the USA that we will advise you. We look forward to working with you over an extended time to facilitate other financial opportunities."

Signed Doctor X PhD.

The foregoing has all of the ingredients of a classic scam. The mystique of dealing in millions of dollars instead of the normal humdrum of only several hundred or even thousand dollars! The opportunity of a lifetime, you may think. Easy money!

"What do I have to lose?" you might say. You only have a relatively small amount of money and a modest savings account, and suddenly you are offered to be catapulted into the big time!

You are wiser than Dr. X, you think. You think that you understand the reasons why the money can only be transferred through a private individual in the US. "After all," you think, "it is from an African country that does not know much about money and is obviously corrupt. What could go wrong? I could become instantly rich!" So you reply, and the hook and line that you have taken begins to reel you in. Naturally you will have to supply the details of your account where the money is to be wired; this will include the ability of the senders having access to your account, your bank manager's name and all pertinent details. You will tell them many things about yourself, and they will tell you nothing substantial about themselves, except for their fax or telephone numbers.

Be sure that when such a large sum is offered there is a reason. And the reason is that they will get a bigger response, especially from people who have modest means. For them to get a two percent response on 100,000 e-mails, means 200 people would respond. An average take per person in fees, goodwill deposits, and outright drawing from each bank account in the amount of say only $1,000, would give them a total take of $200,000! And perhaps much more. This scammer organization is well satisfied with a one or two percent response.]

Scams appeal to our natural tendency toward greed or our desire to get something for nothing. This appeal to the 'something for nothing' mentality is a universal strategy in the scam business. It takes many forms but it is always there—"the great opportunity"—portrayed as something special and usually only avail-able to you!

Soft scams

There are some types of scams that are less clear to positively identify. These types of scams I call "soft scams". This is a real mine-field. The difference between the legitimate and the shady is very thin, as the shady ones also tend to present themselves as worthy people or organizations.

Scam artists can hire sales persons or companies so as to make the process look legitimate. These sales persons, being employed, try to do a good job for their employers, which contributes to the effect-iveness of the scam. This can happen in the soliciting for charities. Some are genuine and some are completely fraudulent.

You are bound to be approached at some time, by mail, phone or in person, to make a gift to a charitable organization. They ask for a donation and they may even offer a small gift as a sign of their appreciation. It is represented that their charitable organization is a very worthwhile organization that does much good. Most people who can afford it enjoy giving to the needy through non-profit charitable organizations that distribute their incoming donations according to certain guidelines. Perhaps you have your own favorite charity. But do you really know how it operates? There are certainly legitimate charitable organizations out there that do a great deal of good in the world. But there are also scammers who want your money and who will go to any lengths to persuade you to give it to them willingly.

Here is how one such scam might possibly work: The phone rings, and an engaging person on the other end tells you that they are soliciting donations for and in behalf of police widows, firemen's widows, or African children who are starving—the list could go on.

They ask you for a small donation, say $50. You say that you cannot afford that amount. They reply, "How much can you afford?" You say "$10". They have got you on the hook! "Thanks," they say, "please confirm it with the supervisor who will shortly come on the line." This is fairly high-pressure soliciting and they are recording your acceptance of giving a donation, to forestall any complaint.

This non-profit organization may be employing from five to twenty people on the phone just to methodically go through the phone directory in your location. These are not usually volunteers—they get paid to solicit you for money! They get paid good wages, sometimes on a commission basis; the more they raise the more their commissions pay. Mind you, you will neither get their physical address nor any contact information, just assurances and thanks for your gift. You may also expect them to put you on their list for calling again next year. Your phone number may also be passed on to another entity for further requests for donations.

These tactics are designed to get your sympathy and to get you to commit to send something. The amounts are relatively small, say $10 to $20, and you think that it is not very much money, yet each solicitor can collect more than $2,500 per week in this way! I base this on an average success donation of $10 as a minimum, ten times each hour, eight hours per day for five days a week. It is easy to see that with a bank of phones in an office and twenty or so people doing the phoning, it would not be hard to gross in excess of $100,000 each week. With an income of $100,000 weekly, that would mean that the head of the organization might make a taxable annual salary of $150,000 or more! Some of what they collect may go to the organization that they are soliciting for, *but how much?* Who is checking their books? The IRS only checks non-profits who gross over a million.

Of course, it is important to recognize that there is a fair amount of expense involved in getting the money from donors. Many people think that because a not-for-profit organization is soliciting your gift then it goes directly to that non-profit and is mostly used for their particular cause, but even legitimate organizations must spend something for overhead. It is a good idea to google the soliciting organization to see how much of the donated money goes to the non-profit organization for operational expenses. Is it 10%, 20%, 50%, or even 75%? This is the acid test! It should be no more than 20% and preferably less. There are quite a few "non-profits" out there that take too much of your donation for their own overheads.

If the operation is registered as a non-profit—meaning there is no taxable profit to the organization—you might think that means they cannot make any profit, which is, strictly speaking, correct. This means that at the end of the year they cannot show a profit from their ongoing operations. All the monies that are collected will be accounted for in some other way. Does the extra money go for high salaries? For a newer building? Or to their cause? A reputable organization publishes a budget or account showing exactly how it spends its income, what is distributed as payments to employees and the head organizers as well as their bonuses, office rent and all the expenses of maintenance and upkeep. Some expenses such as motor vehicle, cell phones, hotel, air travel, and others are deductible as well.

In googling several organizations who had requested me to donate, I found that one seemed to be raising money for an annual fishing trip for the organizations' members! Another one had several reported lawsuits, both inconclusive, and the founder continued to receive a high salary. On the plus side, four or five other organizations proved to be genuine with a large percentage of the donated money going to their cause.

Perhaps you think that for your donation of $10, you are glad to get rid of the solicitation and cannot be bothered to delve into its "nuts and bolts" of its operation, nor can you go to the bother of complaining to the Better Business Bureau. However, if you were making the inquiry you might very well learn that the expenses for the charity were higher than 70% of the total collected!

This type of scam can be avoided by saying to the caller that you never commit to any charity over the phone. If this does not work, then you can insist that you get a copy of their last annual non-profit statement, so that you can verify their legitimacy. Those that solicit donations by phone should be asked to put their information in writing and to send it to you for your consideration. If this is refused, then do not donate. Also look at other factors. For example, if you happen to live in Georgia and a solicitation comes to you for help for Georgian widows, yet they are calling from an address in New Jersey, then something is not right!

Another type of soft scam is time-shares. There is, and has been, a great amount of hype and pressing sales pitches to entice people to buy time-share property. Some people just love to return to a favorite location. It is fine if you want to go for a week or two to the same place at the same time each year for the rest of your lives. Of course, some time-sharing allows for swapping locations, plus owning has a comforting effect. But do you really want to be tied down with what essentially is a second mortgage? If you don't, then time-sharing is not for you.

There are many options which can be an incentive for you to buy. Yet here again, if you will multiply the weekly cost of the time-share by the number of weeks in a year, you will arrive at the total cost of the property; you will be able to see this total is far beyond the realistic value of the overall property. There is the convenience of course if you actually use the time-share. However, the shared upkeep of the property and management fees can be quite high and persistent over the years, and they also tend to increase over time. The commissions paid to the salesmen of the time-shares are extremely high by any standard. The bottom line is that you are the one to pay, and the owner or builder of the property walks away with big profits.

And what happens if you stop using the time-share? Of course you can always give your time-share period away to friends each year, especially as you get older. Quite likely you will be told that you can sell it. Herein lies another difficulty. Let's say after a period of time you decide that you will sell your time-share. You want to sell, but there seems to be a limited number of buyers and lots of sellers. This limits the sales price to something low, but even then it can be hard to sell.

There are many overhead expenses in selling just as in buying. There are the commissions that have to be paid to the selling agent and there are the legal transfer costs that will have to be paid, usually to a lawyer, both of which are high in proportion to the sales price. It is to be expected that the sales price will be low in relation to the original purchase price (inflation adjusted) and your costs are likely to be high in relation to the sales price, possibly as much as 15-20%. Usually you will not know the actual name of the final purchaser. This is because there are professional agents who will buy your time-share just to get it off your hands at a low price, and then resell it to another for a higher price. You will not be aware of this, and even if you were aware, what can you do? By this time you are so glad to get out from under that it will be a great relief for you not to have any more persistent hidden costs. Owning a time-share reminds me of a boat owner's two happiest times: when he buys the boat and when he sells it!

There are some types of mini-scams that involve you buying a special product. They propose that some aspect of your life is at risk and that by using this product, you can become better in health and even live longer!

Maybe I am too skeptical, and quite honestly such products can be very hard to resist. Who of us would not like to be healthier and live longer, or look forever young? It is very natural for each of us to want to feel better, think better, work better, remember better, learn better, overcome tiredness or lethargy, be more productive, earn more money, be happier and more contented, and the list goes on!

Undoubtedly some of these products can make a modest difference in your health, but beware of those that either promise too much, or do not show any real evidence. It may be that there is some basis for their belief that what they are offering is of benefit. Who would dispute that exercise machines can be good for our bodies, that certain vitamin supplements are helpful, or that reading about new developments enhances our knowledge and intelligence? The problem arises when such is hyped up as the only cure, usually exclusively. So much so that you will be "pleased to get this new product at a bargain price"—perhaps several hundred percent greater than its worth (even if there is no worth at all.) People who tout such products often use over-enhanced, influencing words to promote what they are selling.

There are certain sensational phrases and over-selling tactics that are frequently used in these kinds of deceptive sales tactics. The following are some that I have picked out, out of the hundreds that are used:

- "You think you have tried everything—"
- "Doctors hate this—"
- "Most people don't know that—"
- "...will change your life!"
- "I can't state strongly enough—"
- "100% risk free"
- Amazing results in only...
- You'll never....again!
- "I didn't believe it at first, but..."
- "Secret!" Ask yourself, *Why would this wonderful discovery be a secret?*
- "Act now! We cannot guarantee this offer will be repeated." Why not? Because you don't want to stand by your product? Is your firm going to disappear?
- "The one weird trick that can fix almost any health problem!" Really? Sounds too good to be true.
- "Why drug stores and doctors hate this product." How can they hate it when they probably don't know anything about it?

Another example:

- Reprint from "The New England Journal of Modern Medicine"—this got my attention, because it's verifiable, so I checked that journal's online archives, but couldn't find the article "Volume 87 Number 5". Then realized I was checking the archives of the "New England Journal of Medicine." There is NO New England Journal of MODERN Medicine online. The scammers slipped that word in to fool us, the public. Not to mention that the "article" itself was not as scholarly as one might expect, containing claims of "huge implications" and "numerous [unnamed] trials"

The list of meaningless over statements goes on, and new ones are being put forward as the circumstances warrant. Often it isn't just what is said, but how it is said. Promises are made, results are exaggerated, there's no risk to you and you can pay in a series of affordable installments. Be wary of words that promise a lot and tell you nothing about the real value of the product you are buying. It's easy to manipulate words in order to make you believe something has been said that really hasn't. And everything, even a watch that is only right two times a day, has some value. Just be sure that, when you are at last persuaded to part with your money, it's for something that has real value to you and you haven't simply been manipulated by clever marketing techniques.

Of course, all advertisements for health supplements add *if's, but's, maybe's, could's* and *perhaps's,* etc, since no positive claims can be made without FDA approval. And, in fact, the FDA forbids any supplement to claim a total cure for any medical problem, as this is strictly the domain of medical doctors. That doesn't mean such claims are inherently false, but it doesn't mean they are true, either. Being slightly cynical and thinking in a critical way can be helpful for sorting through the avalanche of information that comes to you verbally and visually. I also add that you critique at a moderate level because to become a total cynic would preclude you from finding things out that you need to know. Getting to where you automatically think through what you hear and read takes time. We humans are a naturally believing group and I think it sad that we have to struggle so hard to filter out truth from half-truth, yet half-truths have been perpetuated since the start of mankind's existence and learning to filter such things out is a skill that should be learned as soon as possible—and practiced often.

Conclusion

There are so many ways that you and I can be scammed that it would take several large books to recount them. We need not go into all the various ways that you can be taken in. All you have to remember is that anyone you meet has the potential to scam you, and that when opportunities come your way you should put your consequential thinking cap on and look at all of the possibilities that it might be a scam. Nice though the scammers may be, the nicer and the more genuine they are, the more the likelihood of you losing out. Always be on your guard until you absolutely know that it is a false alarm. And if others around you are taken in by a scam, still do not participate. Just because others whom you may respect are taken in does not mean that you have to join them, even if for the short term you are accused of being in the wrong!

Scamming will continue to happen, notwithstanding laws to try to prevent such abuses. Human nature is still the same. Scammers of all creeds, genders and persuasions will continue to invent new and innovative ways to get your hard-earned money. Your responsibility to yourself is to recognize a scam's key ingredients and show them up for what they are and not to be taken by them.

I end this chapter with one of the latest scams I have come across. The person involved suffered severely. Yet it was a scam that was hard to resist, as it really did give the money that it promised.

Imagine that you are enticed to help a friend of a friend (who in reality is only an acquaintance) who will be going abroad for an extended period of time. This person does not want you to pay him, he wants to pay you—ten percent of his income!

His income, which comes to him in the form of dollars, needs a U.S. recipient as this person will be overseas for a period of time and be unable to have the money automatically redirected. He needs someone (you) to wire the funds received to him at his overseas address which is a bank or other non-definite address. It is hinted that the funds are partly royalty income. There will be variable amounts deposited into your bank account from various sources. Any taxes will be taken care of by incoming monies. Your job is to wire it into a given overseas account, subtracting ten percent for you! You are told that the sums will be substantial. Great, you think! How could I possibly lose?

Collecting these sums and forwarding them on would seem to be a no-brainer to anyone. However asking, "Is this too good to be true?" reveals the likelihood of a scam. More especially because it appears that there are no risks. Now is the time to apply your consequential thinking!

You should ask some questions and get some facts. First of all, why you? You do not personally know the person who is going abroad for two years, so again, why you? Secondly, you are told not to worry about taxes at all, as these are taken care of. Why is this? Is it because they don't want you to dig too deeply? Finally, what can go wrong? Think long and hard about this one. You get the money, but what can go wrong if you do get the money?

Why the secrecy? You are not told the nature of the payments to be made, just that they will come from several sources. You are not told the names of the people sending the money. You are to wire the balance of the funds received to a bank account, usually in dollars, but otherwise you have no actual address of this person who will receive the money.

Here is what actually happened. The money started coming in, lots of it—some thousands of dollars, all of which was duly wired to the designated bank account, less the ten percent. The receiver thought that he was onto a very good thing and wanted it to continue for the full two years. However, he started having these strange e-mails asking where the purchased product was. Initially he ignored these as wayward junk mail, but these e-mails escalated over the next two months and got more threatening.

Finally he had a summons charging him with falsifying sales of goods, keeping the money and refusing to deliver the goods promised. He was liable for all of the money that he had sent to this person abroad, who was unreachable and untraceable! It had looked too good to be true, and it certainly was! Unknown to the receiver, the man overseas had been selling false goods in the U.S. and had gotten the receiver to process the monies for the goods in a way that would protect the scammer. The money had been sent to this man overseas away from the law and away from the people who had sent the money for goods. The one who looked bad in the eyes of the law was—himself! He learned the hard way—don't allow your greed to be the master over your common sense.

CHAPTER FOUR

Negotiation: Its Art and Power

No one wants to pay more than they have to for any given item. You have only to go to China or the Middle East, perhaps Morocco or India to find that the art of negotiation is carried on throughout the world to various degrees of perfection. No one wants to pay more than they have to for any given item. In ,many countries, trying to get the best price is an expected way of buying, selling and doing business. Even in Europe and the U.S., where retail prices are firm, negotiating for large purchases like houses, cars, and jewelry is acceptable, even expected. Such is a fact of life, and by learning to negotiate you will be able to get farther ahead than you normally could without this skill.

The factors influencing negotiation price

The extent to which you will be able to negotiate a price lower than initially offered will depend on various factors:

The weather: I have often gone to a sale and found that the weather has affected either the increase or decrease of the cost of the items to be sold; this is because of supply and demand. Take, for example, an auction sale where you bid on particular items you want. If you find that there has just been some heavy snow or rain, or if it is in the middle of a heat wave, then you can expect that the number of people attending the auction will be less than under normal conditions. There are always some people who would have attended but decide not to go when conditions are not conducive to their health or general comfort.

For these reasons there might be fewer bidders for any given item, and this would reduce the bidding competition. Thus the items would command a lesser price than otherwise. You see, fewer bidders means, in effect, less demand and more supply which tends to drive prices down. Conversely, if there are lots of bidders, this creates more demand and causes the ending sale price to be higher than it might have been otherwise.

The time of year: There is a tendency for certain items, such as homes and real estate, to fetch a higher price in the spring. The reason for this is that there is a greater demand in the spring, caused by the fact that people prefer to move when it has the least impact on their children's education. In the Northern Hemisphere, October through April are the least preferred times to move, and prices for houses during this time are lower due to lower demand.

Scarcity: Items that are in short supply always command higher prices. For example, diamonds are very scarce and because of this they command very high prices. Another example is vintage cars. When first manufactured they are relatively cheap; yet after eighty years the ones that are left, being not very many, command very high prices if they have been well maintained. Also, there are certain painters whose works of art are very much sought after and command very high prices. And why do they command such high prices? Because there are few available for purchase compared to the demand for them! And so you see, price is often dictated by supply and demand.

All in all, knowing the degree of scarcity or abundance of an item will enable you to make appropriate offers when buying or to fix your asking price at the right spot when selling.

Being perceived as rich or poor: When buying, you must never give the impression that you are well off. If you do, the seller will tend to increase their selling price or at the very least be more reluctant to reduce it. It is natural that we humans want to sell something at a higher price to someone who has the money, and the reverse is true when selling to someone whom we perceive as poor.

If you are the seller you also do not want to give the impression that you are well off. If you do so it will only work against you. The buyer will likely wonder why you are selling and may consider your offered price too high because they perceive that you can afford to sell it for less. Because of this, the potential buyer will try to get a lower price than he might otherwise have expected. Basically, it all comes down to common sense and what you would naturally do in similar circumstances.

Humility: Being humble can pay off sometimes. You must never come across as superior to the seller, even if you think you are. Being humble will get you farther in almost any negotiation. This is because a person who comes across as humble is not threatening to the other person. A humble person is relatively easy to deal with. None of us like to do business or negotiate with a brash or aggressive person. "Gently does it" will keep them friendly towards you, to your benefit. There is nothing underhanded about trying to be humble. The people who are not able to be humble at least on some occasions, I am convinced, will lead a less productive life.

Being liked: It is best if the seller likes you; being liked is necessary in order to get the best deal. However, if the seller is desperate to sell they are probably so pleased that you are interested in buying that they like you no matter what; that is, unless you start taking undue advantage of them which you should not do.

I think that it is a human trait that we all appreciate being liked. In any working relationship being liked is paramount. Have you noticed that it is hard to have problems with someone who likes you? Two people who get along well can get so much more accomplished between them. This is why buyers should always try to be friendly to the seller and attempt to like the seller as much as possible in the circumstances. Gaining a friend is harder than gaining an enemy, but gaining an enemy would clearly be counterproductive in all circumstances and especially in business dealings. Friendliness denotes the willingness to compromise; because of this, when both the seller and buyer like each other they will be able to work out the best deal. Also, each will walk away happy to have finished the deal on some level of friendship.

It is unfortunate but I have noticed that many people profess to dislike others, often with very little reason. Making a resolve to like others is not only positive but necessary in any business. Of course there will be those who do or say things that make it hard to like them or who you find you just cannot get along with. In these cases, do not feel you have to do business with them. If you do business with someone that you just cannot like, you will be opening the door for later problems.

Type of seller or buyer they are: We must not forget the particular type of person that you have to deal with. This is another con-sequential-thinking operation that will help you assess the whole situation. The type of buyer or seller that you have to deal with is very important to figure out, and knowing this will help you get the best deal. If you know nothing about them, it is a good idea to try to find out, if you can, what others think about them without being pushy about it.

Some questions to ask yourself about them are: are they reasonably-minded people? Do they have a reputation for underhanded or un-ethical dealings? Could they be a scammer? Are they in need or possibly having money troubles? This latter question can be a problem, as you do not want to take advantage of them (I hope) and on the other hand you do not want them to take advantage of you either. It is a somewhat delicate balance between several factors, the most important of which is, do you feel comfortable about the deal?

If you suspect that they are not what they portray themselves to be, back away from the deal. You want a good deal, not any deal. Going into an agreement, even a good financial one, will in the end turn out badly if it is found that the seller or buyer was not an honest or reasonable person. It is not possible to get a good agreement from a bad person, because they will be out to get you in any way possible. That is why it is important to know what kind of person they are before doing a deal with them.

Keenness to buy or sell: The keenness of the seller and their need to sell is always an important factor if you are trying to get the best price. If they are ardent about selling something, you will be able to get it at a lower price than if they are not eager for the sale. Usually, when a seller has a lot to sell there is a reason; they want to dispose of something they have. Supply and demand is involved here. When a person is keen to sell something, it is the equivalent of the supply going up, resulting in a lower price.

Getting something at a lower price has nothing to do with taking advantage of another person. They want to sell because of their circumstances and needs, which may be many and varied, and you are where you are because of your circumstances. Therefore, you are willing and able to buy only *if the price is right* for you. Everyone likes a bargain. That is the way most of us think.

You yourself must never seem to be extremely keen to purchase or sell. If you do, then you will pay more or get less than you might have done. The more you increase your demand for something, the more (theoretically) you are willing to pay for it. The seller will be able to sense this, and will hold out in order to get you to pay more.

Your emotions: Emotion has no place in successful negotiation. Your emotional state at the time of any negotiation needs to be kept very much under control. To cry if you are selling puts the buyer under some hesitation to purchase what you have to sell. To get excited when you are buying alerts the buyer to raise the price. A calm, unruffled and unemotional negotiation will bring you the best results, besides which you will be able to think more clearly.

There was a time when I was urgently looking for some suitable land to operate a business. I located some marshy land near a river estuary in the outer suburbs of Sydney, Australia. The land was low lying, but not normally subject to flooding. It looked terrible because it had been neglected for a long time, but its location was ideal, and the acreage was fine at five acres. I thought I would be able fix it up in order to have it meet my needs. It was not listed for sale; however, I located the owners who happened to be a large food company. I took the "bull by the horns" as it were, phoned the company and asked to speak to the general manager. I was new at this type of thing and was rather nervous. Nevertheless, I made an appointment to see him.

At our meeting I indicated that I wanted to start a small business on the land, producing mushroom spawn for the Australian mushroom industry. He was intrigued by this plan of mine. He could see that I was at the beginning of a new venture. He asked me how much I would be willing to offer. I said that I could not go above 6,000 Australian pounds (the currency of the time) and would prefer to give less. I have to tell you at this juncture that I was still in my twenties. I had only once negotiated for the purchase of land before. I was somewhat out of my depth too because it was a big company, the man was 35–40 years older than me, and he was the top man, the general manager. But I was honest and direct, and to my good fortune the manager liked me.

There is no doubt in my mind that he was being kind to this young, energetic lad who had a limited amount of money. He probably knew that the land was worth more, yet owned by a large corporation that had no use for it. He smiled and said that the land in question was surplus to his company's requirements and that if I would put in writing an offer for 5,000 Australian pounds, he would put it to the board members and possibly my offer would be accepted. Within two weeks I had a letter from the company stating that I could purchase the land for an agreed price of 5,000 Australian pounds!

I was young, but I did not try to play games. I told this man the truth, which he could well see with his many years of experience in business. It was a kind thing for him to do, to give assistance to a young, up-and-coming entrepreneur like myself. This experience shaped my understanding that people in business, even in high positions, can be kind people. The managing director thought, and rightly so, that I needed a helping hand—in other words he liked my honest approach and attitude. And I was proud of the fact that my emotions were always under control, they were always straightforward and direct, which allowed me to have a professional approach with the managing director and ultimately get the land for a price that I could afford.

Another part of not letting emotions get involved is not to be aggressive. There is an analogy that well teaches how to avoid the negative effects of aggression. Imagine a sailing ship on the ocean of life. When the wind blows, or is the aggressor, it makes the ship move; but if the ship takes down all of its sails, then the wind has little effect. On the other hand, if the sailing ship is the aggressor, with sails full, and the wind dies down, the ship cannot move any more. So it is in human relations. In business when buying, selling or negotiating, you need to take the attitude of not allowing the wind to get in your sails, and not contributing to or reacting to aggression. In this way you will be able to avoid an unfriendly situation. Remember, "It takes two to tango!"

Specific ways to negotiate for different items

Houses: In the Northern Hemisphere the best time to sell a home is in the spring, from March through June; the worst time to sell a home is in the autumn, from August through December. This is in part because of the demand factor, as mentioned before. The prices which sellers can obtain are higher in the spring than in the autumn, generally by an order of 15%, or $15,000 out of every $100,000 of sale price. Not an inconsiderable sum of money!

Conversely, it is best to buy a home in the autumn months. Of course this is not always possible, because it is first normally necessary to sell your home before buying another.

Where houses are concerned, everyone wants to sell their home for the best price possible. The house seller should have a good idea as to what the selling price should be which will depend on the location, quality, square footage, and the state of the housing economy. This figure should then be divided by one hundred and multiplied by one hundred and fifteen; the resulting figure becomes the asking price. By adding 15% to the price, you then have room for negotiation.

If you offer your property at what you want to sell it for right at the beginning, you cannot normally expect to get it because you will be beaten down to some lower price. Unless you raise your price higher than you actually want, you will be dissatisfied to some extent. You need to realize that it is very seldom that the first asking price, or first offer prices, are realized. There is mostly some sort of compromise between the two, so that the final price is satisfactory to both parties (buyer and seller) and a mutually acceptable deal is reached.

96

It is normally best to sell property through a real estate agent, and they can be negotiated with for a 20% to 30% reduction in their selling fees by giving them exclusive selling rights or other incentives such as giving them more properties to sell for you. Another way to deal with the fees is to adjust your original selling price to include the realtor fees in it (but don't tell the realtor that).

Just as those who are selling a house want the highest price possible, those who are buying want to buy at the lowest price possible. When a home is found that the buyer is interested in purchasing, in order to get the best price the buyer should divide the asking price by one hundred and then multiply it by eighty-five. This then becomes the offer price. This price will normally be rejected outright and will be countered with another price that the seller will offer.

If, when negotiating for a house or any other item for that matter, the seller immediately accepts your offer, be wary. They are usually either very desperate to sell or what you are buying is not what it is purported to be! The buyer usually makes a counter offer by raising their bid by about 5%. Now the seller might consider this new price and accept, or perhaps counter the offer again with a suggestion to split the difference between the new offer and the last offered price to buy. The offer and counter offers eventually come to a price acceptable to both parties, even if the middle point might be a little off center.

Just for the sake of showing how this might work, here is a hypo-thetical example: Let us take a case where a seller would like to sell their home for a fair price of, say, $200,000. First the seller divides by one hundred and multiplies by one hundred and fifteen to get 15% above their wanted price, resulting in an asking price of $230,000. The buyer comes along and after taking an interest in the home's purchase, quietly divides the asking price by 100 and multiplies the answer by 85, resulting in a new figure of $195,500. This becomes their offer price. When this offer by the buyer is compared to the seller's initial desired price of $200,000 (before the $30,000 was added on), the seller of the property is within $5,000, but naturally they say nothing. The seller of the property now openly counters the buyer's first offer with a reduction in their price by 5% (which is

$11,500) to a new asking price of $218,500 (now it is $18,500 above their original wanted price). The buyer could reject this counter price, and would normally make another counter offer, this time raising their offer by $5,000 or about 2 and 1/2% (it could be more, but remember, one can always go higher, but never lower); this would make their new offer $200,500. The seller could accept this new offer, depending on circumstances and feelings. But if I were the seller, I would tell the buyer that much as I am reluctant to do so, I will split the difference with them; that is, split the exact difference between my last selling price offer and the buyer's newest offer. The new price offered would then be $209,250, or halfway between the $218,500 and $200,000. The potential buyer might well accept the new offer of reduction, but if I were the buyer, I might consider proposing an offer of splitting the difference between my offer of $200,000 and the seller's compromise of $209,250. Like a double compromise! Such an offer would be the middle point of the two figures, or, in this case, $204,625. It sounds complicated, yet with a small hand-held calculator it is not. As the buyer, if I got the house at my new offered price of $204.625, fine. If not, then I would (outwardly reluctantly) accept the last offered price of $209,250.

Do you see that the end result is pleasant to both buyer and seller? The seller has more than the original price thought acceptable to them (before the 15% upwards adjustment) and the purchaser has succeeded in getting a reduction in the original asking price of just over twenty thousand dollars! So there are happy feelings all around.

You might think that all this play is not worth the trouble. But to have a win-win situation is always worth the trouble. A lifetime of such actions will translate into a huge financial benefit to both parties.

This is the way it is done. You both end up at a price that you are prepared to sell or to buy. If a seller wants to sell at too high a price, the seller will not find a buyer. If a buyer wants to buy at an unrealistically low price, the buyer will not be able to buy. Much of the foregoing is due to supply and demand. Ask yourself if it is a seller's or a buyer's market. A seller's market means that the market is to the advantage of the seller, because the prices are right for selling. A buyer's market is just the opposite. (You can find out if it is a buyer's or seller's market by calling a realtor.) All these things must be taken into account. Finally, to wait for property prices to go lower is a recipe for not finding anything now and having to pay much more in the future. Due to inflation, the price of houses in the long term tends to rise, as covered in the "Money and Inflation" chapter, Chapter One.

As passing advice to a potential buyer, here's a word of warning: If your partner is looking at a home you both might live in, tell them beforehand to keep a straight face and say nothing about what they like about the property, such as "Ooh, what a lovely ____,"or some such exclamation. The seller will naturally want to show off the best features of the home with all of its many advantages, hoping that it will persuade the buyer to buy, but if you or your partner like it, you should not show this too keenly. Such obvious enthusiasm will likely cost you in the negotiation process. Tell your partner to have a pad and to write down their thoughts so that you can discuss them later.

Motor vehicles: In purchasing motor vehicles, almost the sky is the limit in relation to how much the seller will ask, probably because asking prices are way more than what the seller thinks that they will get. The price is often unrelated to the car's worth or condition. There is the old saying (similar to when buying jewelry) which is, "let the buyer beware"—in other words, it is up to the buyer to beware of the sales people and the condition of the car. Buying from a dealer, both new cars and used, can be daylight robbery if you are not very careful.

I have purchased many new and used cars in my time, and learned many lessons. For my children, I have learned that second-hand cars can be either a blessing if they run well or the opposite if they don't. However, I have seldom overpaid, though in truth, no car is truly a bargain because of how fast they depreciate and how much maintenance they need if they are not to fall apart quickly.

In the case of a used car, you likely won't know who owned it before, how it was kept up (though if you can get a maintenance history on the car, that is a plus), or what condition it was in before you purchased it, notwithstanding what the salesperson tells you. If a second-hand dealer will put everything they say about the car in writing and guarantee the reliability, this could be OK. Nevertheless, I have found that it's better to buy a used car from a new-car dealership. This is what I usually do. When new-car dealerships get a used car (usually from trade-ins), it is always examined closely by experts to see if there is a problem. If there is one, it is fixed by their service department before it is sold—brakes, lights, etc. They try to make sure everything is right, because their reputation is on the line. Reputable new-car dealerships will not knowingly sell lemons.

It is best not to use a trade-in when buying a car. It is far better to sell your trade-in vehicle privately, even if the dealer does offer you a better price than you think you can sell it for. This is because without the trade-in you will likely be able to get a much lower price for the vehicle you are buying. You see, even with a trade-in, it is the car you are buying that makes money for the seller. An increase in the offered price for your trade-in will only result in a higher price for your purchased car. It is like a juggling match, with the two prices keeping the same distance apart. (Buying a new car with a trade-in or a used car with a trade-in works basically the same way.) Also, perhaps you are aware that the price that a car dealer will pay for your trade-in is normally a good deal less than the price for which he will later attempt to sell it. The amount for which he will try to sell it translates into a little less than double what he will pay you.

Another important thing to be aware of is that the dealer, to entice you to buy, uses the difference between the original price of the car and what they initially offer it for (the sticker price) as a selling tool. This is demonstrated by something that I actually did some years ago when I was interested in purchasing a car for one of my children, whom I did not take to the dealership with me for the important reason that their enthusiasm for a car would jeopardize my ability to get a good deal.

I went to a major, well respected, new-and-used car dealership and looked over what they had to offer. Amongst many other vehicles, I saw just the one that would be ideal. It was the exact station wagon that I was looking for, a Sable Ford about five years old with 65,000 miles on the clock. It looked in excellent condition, and the sticker price was $6000, less than half the price of a new model.

The friendly salesman came over to see me and asked if I was interested. I told him that I was slightly interested in the station wagon. He said that it was a real bargain at $6,000, such a low price! I said that it looked quite nice but that the price was too high for me. He said, "Make an offer," and, "Do you have a trade-in?" I said that I might have a trade-in but that the car was not in very good condition. He said that he would give me $1,000 for any vehicle I had, sight unseen, and not to worry about the condition of it. This was a sign that he was very keen to make a sale, because he was willing to give $1,000 for a car of which he had no idea of the value or condition. Therefore, without the trade-in I should be able to get the vehicle for $5,000, instead of $6,000.

I then applied my "negotiating for a used car" formula, which is to offer 66% or 2/3 of the asking price. I said that I would offer $4,000 for the vehicle with no trade-in. He threw up his hands and said that it would be impossible. "Right," I said. "See you some other time," and I started to walk away (a very important thing to do!). I had not gone more than fifteen feet when he called out for me to wait a moment while he went to see his manager.

He came back shortly and said that the manager would let me have it for $4,800, just $200 less than the $5,000 that it was worth. "No," I said, "but I will make a new offer of $4,200." I came up only $200, 5% on the $4,000 because I wanted to leave myself room to continue negotiating, moving up little by little. I was quite prepared to pay $5,000 if I had to, because I really liked the car—but I didn't tell him that. "No," he said, "the manager said that it was the lowest possible price." "OK," I said, "I will see you, good-bye." I started to walk away again. "No, wait a minute," he said, "I will see my manager again." He came back and said that his manager said that after looking at all factors regarding the car and that I looked to be a good guy, and that it was getting near the end of the month for sales, etc., he would let me have it for $4,500. "No," I said, "but reluctantly I will be prepared to split the difference, a cash deal for $4,350, and that is positively my last offer." (In general, if you pay cash, you'll get a better deal. As they say, "Cash is king.") "Oh," the salesman said, "you drive a very hard bargain, I'll go and see the manager, but I do not think he will take it, why not make it a round $4,400?" "No," I said, "$4,350 or nothing!"

You might be wondering why I balked at paying another $50. I knew that if their price was firm at $4,400 or even $4,500, and that I had finally exhausted their selling powers, I could always come back later and say that after all, I would buy it for their lowest price. Needless to say, the salesman came back to say that I could have it, but that he had had to forego his normal commission. Sob story from a car salesman! I did not believe that either.

Interestingly, after driving it for two days locally, I found that there were certain faults: a tire had a bad slit on the inside, the windshield washer did not work, and the car had a tendency to steer to the left. These were all rather small items, yet annoying, so I took it back and saw the sales manager in person. I told him of my complaints and pointed out to him that some of the faults could have caused an accident which could have rebounded on the dealership, and that I expected him to fix the problems. If he had refused, I would've said I wanted my money back. I did so in a straightforward way without emotion, important in these types of dealings. He quickly apologized, said that he was unaware of the various faults and would fix them at no charge to me. Some dealers may want to add an "As-is" or "No Cool-Off" clause to the contract. Beware and don't sign a contract like that, not for a used car. Too much can go wrong.

There is an important point I want to make here: I did not go and buy a second-hand car from a side street dealer, nor one that had no repair shop. If I had, once I had taken the car off their selling lot, I would have had little ability to have anything corrected when I had a legitimate complaint. New car dealerships generally have a reputation to uphold, otherwise word gets around and their business suffers. For businesses like these, losing a customer is easy and getting one back is difficult.

When purchasing a used vehicle you always want to start out by offering 2/3 of the sticker price. You could even start with 1/2 of the sticker price! After all, what harm does it do to try? And it is important to walk away if the salesman is not willing to negotiate. Once the salesman is willing to negotiate, you gradually work up from your initial offer bit by bit over time as the salesman works down bit by bit from their price until you have a price that basically meets somewhere in the middle. If at any time they are not prepared to negotiate anymore, and you haven't yet reached that middle point, you should be prepared to walk away. This will give you the upper hand. After all, if you decide a day or two later that you are prepared to pay the last price that was offered, you can always go back and ask them for it. However, it is important to relate that I've often had the salesman call me up after I had walked away and gone home (generally within 24 hours) in order to offer me a lower price or to ask to get together again to nail down a price. Sometimes they'll ask if you've thought over the price, in which case you say that you still think it's too high (you do not want to show them a chink in your armor).

Finally, if you ever buy a used car from a used-car dealership (which I do not recommend) make sure the dealer, by way of the person you are dealing with, puts in writing anything they say about the car, good or bad. With new-car dealerships you do not need to do this. An example of something you might want to put in writing is, "We stand behind the reliability of this car for three (or six) months from the date of purchase." Also, get a mechanic or Triple A to come and look the car over. If the dealer is offended by this and doesn't let you bring someone in to check it, then they likely have something to hide and you probably shouldn't buy from them.

The purchase of a new vehicle is a somewhat different matter than the purchase of a used car, though the principles of negotiation are the same. The price ticket that you see posted on a new car, like with used cars, can always be negotiated downwards by you, with few exceptions. The main difference is simply that the amount you can negotiate down is less.

In general, the initial price that you should first offer for a new vehicle is 15%–25% less than the sticker price for a new-year model and 20–30% less than the sticker price for a year-old model. What percentage you take off exactly and the price you will finally be able to get depend on many things: How badly do you want the particular car? If you are casual, you can offer less. If you are particularly interested you might offer more. How long has the model been on the market? Don't hesitate to ask. The longer it has been on the market, the older the model is, and the easier it will be to get a lower price. For example, end of a model year cars (the cars that are left over) are always sold at a lower price than the new next year's model that has just come out. Current year models that are not all over their yard are generally harder to get a reduction on because they are in short supply. Another question is, are you asking for anything special? If you are requesting the dealership to get a specially fitted car delivered according to your particular wishes, you will have a harder time getting a reduction in the price. Also, is the car in great demand? If yes, this will mean you'll have to pay more. For example, a hot-selling vehicle with special features has a price tag that is less negotiable. Finally, are you paying cash? If you pay cash you will be able to get the car for less. So as you can see, the exact price you will be able to get depends on several factors. The final price will also depend on the quality and sticker price of the new car together with the time of the year—all cars tend to be offered at a higher price in the spring and a lower one in the autumn. The percentages are only a guide. And in the end, don't be afraid to walk away. If the salesman thinks he's got you, then you're in trouble.

When negotiating, always check to see if there are any special discounts from the dealer or manufacturer on the car you want, and take this into account by offering a price that is a little lower than you would have normally offered with the formula. Also, look at the mileage on the car; 500-1,000 is plenty. If the car is over 1,000 miles, negotiate a lower price; sometimes dealers will use new cars for their own personal or dealership use before trying to sell it later as a new car, yet the car may have up to 20,000 miles on the clock!

For a dealer to sell a brand new model vehicle in the region of two-thirds of the recommended sticker sale price is not at all unusual. Of course, the game plan for the dealership alters from year to year; the manufacturers give certain incentives to their dealerships that often determine the price the dealership pays for the car that will in turn determine how much they are willing to negotiate. The automakers often offer special bonuses and discounts to the dealership at the end of each model year, like in the fall or late summer, in order to clear out the old, unsold models. And so what model of car it is and what year it is will change the price in a subtle way between what you would normally have to pay and what you will ultimately be able to negotiate.

Dealerships have a dealership price that they always pay to the manufacturer, but sometimes there are two dealership prices: one for a large dealership (which would contain a bigger discount) and one for a small dealership (which would be a smaller discount). Sometimes there are even additional promotional discounts that are used to help move the manufacturer's surplus inventory of cars. As said before, the dealer, in order to entice the buyer to buy, uses the difference between what they paid and what they initially offer it for as a selling tool. Some will even tell you that you can have the vehicle for just $200 above their factory invoice price with no trade-in. Do not fall for this, as there is often a two-tiered invoice price, one before any factory discounts and one after!

Depending on your financial situation, a dealership will often encourage you to buy a new vehicle by explaining to you that they can finance it at an exceptionally low rate. I had a friend once who was taken in by this type of sales pitch and was tricked into paying top dollar for a vehicle on a five-year terms purchase at 2%, which was bound to cause problems for him later, because in spite of the low rate, or actually because of it, he was forced to pay a non-discounted price for the car. When you buy "on terms" you end up paying more than you otherwise would. Also the insurance on the car is higher because the insurance company has to insure the lien holder as well (the people who financed the purchase of the car). Anyone who buys on terms pays a higher insurance because of the two owners, them and the lien holder. My friend was locked into paying a large amount each month as the car quickly decreased in value—new cars decrease in price by approximately one third during the first year. He was locked into a purchase where at any one time during the five-year purchase, the vehicle was worth less than the amount of the loan.

Had he asked me what to do, I could have saved him probably $6,000 by first negotiating the price and then afterwards negotiating the terms (as well as a trade-in if necessary). It would have been much better for him to have financed the car through a bank rather than the car dealership because he could then have offered to pay cash for the car, which would have allowed him to negotiate a lower price for it. The situation he got himself into caused him a deal of grief later. Getting a new vehicle has a tremendous pull on people; it just feels good to have a new car! They act in haste and repent at leisure.

Be very careful of a sales pitch like, "We have a special on at the moment, *zero finance charges for up to three years!*" The catch here is that you might be so in love with getting a new car with no interest charges that you lose sight of the fact that you will be paying top dollar for the vehicle that otherwise you could have probably purchased for many thousands of dollars less!

Jewelry: Jewelry is an item that people generally think of as being worth more than it really is. Yet having said this, what any given item is worth ultimately depends on the value to that person, even if it does not have the same value to another. This is why bidding on jewelry can be hazardous. In general, offering 10% to 20% less if it is a private jeweler in the US is a good starting point, and half of what is being asked if it is a jeweler in an overseas country. The higher the price, the bigger the discount you can normally get. In dealing with a large company jewelry store in the US, such as are found in malls, the same is usually not possible, but there is no harm in asking if they have a special sales promotion.

When at a jewelry shop, showing an interest is fine if you intend to buy something, but the prices should be realistic and within your budget. An indication to the seller that you are interested but think that it is beyond your budget will often result in your being offered a lower price. If this is still too much, wait, and just as you are about to move on an even lower price might be offered. This latter approach, of further and further price reduction, is more likely to happen when traveling abroad. The sales agent will not think the worse of you for trying to get the object at a lower price, either. Remember, do not seem too anxious to purchase. This is fatal for your pocket! And don't forget to be careful about taking others with you who would show too much interest. If they reveal that they like or want the item, you can expect to pay a higher price. Mind you, it takes some level of discipline to resist the skills of a good sales person. After all, that is why they are there, and if they do not sell, their sales position is at risk.

Many times when buying jewelry from a dealer or a jewelry store anywhere in the world, they will expound on the value of diamonds, precious stones, gold, silver and specially crafted items. This is quite natural when you consider that they are in business to sell. Just try to sell them some of your grandmother's old jewelry and watch their response. They will not want to buy it unless it is very advantageous to them i.e., they know they can sell it for considerably more than the price you sell it to them, because they are in the business to sell at a profit not to buy for a loss.

Gold, diamonds and other special stones are notorious for having their initial asking prices heavily inflated, usually by more than 100%—double or even three times the true value. If you hesitate to believe this, then why do you occasionally see special sales with offers of "30% off marked prices"? On a $1,500 item, this would mean that a sale price of $1,000 would still be acceptable to the seller. Such inflated pricing is not so outrageous when you take into account that such shops have quite heavy financial overheads. Their aim is not only to stay in business but also to be able to pay all expenses and bonuses to their sales staff. This is a normal part of running a business. However, this should not detract the purchaser from attempting to get a better deal.

Furniture: When buying household furniture, there are often good opportunities to get a better deal, even if it is a recognized retail business. Second-hand dealers are the easiest place to get a good deal. Getting a lesser price of 5–35% is usually possible, depending on how many items you are planning on buying and how much the total cost will be.

In general, the higher the price and the more pieces of furniture you are looking for, the more discount can be negotiated. In addition, ask for free delivery of the purchases to your home. If you can, put a cash deposit on your purchases with a promise to pay the balance in cash upon delivery. You don't pay for it all right away because you want to wait until you get it safely and without damage before you pay; that way you have leverage with them if things go wrong. Of course, by paying with your credit card, you also have some leverage because if things go wrong, you can call the credit card company and ask them to reverse the charge. But by paying the deposit in cash, you will get their keen interest to please you and give you a good deal! Bargaining can be fun as well as cost effective.

Negotiating bank foreclosures and contractor fees

Bank foreclosures: I once purchased a home from a bank foreclosure where the original purchaser had put a 5% deposit down to buy the home and persuaded the bank to finance the rest. Later, the original owner had to relocate to another state. In desperation to sell quickly, the original owner found a buyer who was willing to buy the home on terms, unconnected to the bank that had originally lent the money. The deal for the seller seemed good. It took care, so the seller thought, of the mortgage payments, the taxes, the maintenance charges and the upkeep of the garden. However, the modest down payment of two thousand dollars to be paid by the new buyer only represented the equivalent of one month's rent. While the buyers seemed nice, the actual fact was that for the seller the deal was terrible.

It just so happened that the newest purchaser was a dog lover. He had six of them, and each night the dogs were placed in the basement of the home. Eventually the heating and air conditioning systems were ripped out by the dogs, the plaster walls were torn apart, the downstairs door was ruined with scratches, and the carpet was ripped up in several places. Within one year the whole interior of the basement was severely damaged and neglected. In addition, after the initial down payment, the new purchasers didn't pay anything more. After finding out how the purchasers had trashed the property, the owner gave up and walked away from the home, which left the bank to pick up the pieces as they now became the new owner by default. The bank, in turn, was looking to get rid of it at almost any price. I heard of it through a realtor and made an offer of just about half the going price for a similar home in the area, thinking that I could fix the problems and renovate the home. My offer was negotiated slightly higher and then I was able to buy it.

Bank foreclosures are fairly straightforward to negotiate. A bank will find itself owning property that it does not want because the original owners have defaulted. Banks are generally not in the business of owning property and unless there is some compelling reason to keep it, they will bend over backwards to dispose of it. However, generally there is a minimum price for which they are prepared to sell the property, meaning they will not sell lower than that price, unless there are extenuating circumstances such as too many properties on their books or higher than normal maintenance costs.

When negotiating, first you should try to get the bank to come down in their asking price by making an offer that is 5-10% lower and see what happens. Sometimes they will take it and sometimes they won't, but you lose nothing by trying. If they don't, it may be because the bank has a certain price below which they cannot sell the house. You'll know this is the case if they won't yield in their price. Then you have to decide if the price they want is acceptable to you.

Regardless of what happens with negotiating the price, the terms can always be negotiated, including interest rates, down payment, when the payments will start, etc. It is in the area of terms and interest that banks really are familiar. It looks good on a bank's balance sheet that they have mortgage or loan accounts with good, reliable customers. After you settle on the price of the house, then propose the interest rate and length of time that you are prepared to pay. Begin by asking for the prime rate of interest (the rate that banks lend to other banks and very good customers), no payments for one year, and a payment length of 15 years or more. Depending on your situation, getting a loan for the purchase of the property at the prime interest rate, or even one point above, would be satisfactory. How good an interest rate you get depends on the national interest rate and your credit history.

Assuming the property is being purchased as an investment, you'll want to take out a business loan. In such a case you want to pay as little cash up front as possible so that you can put your money into improvements and pay the bank mostly when the house is resold. The longer the time you have to pay back the loan, the less the amount of your monthly payments and thus you will be able to preserve your capital for your expenditures. You may pay the loan off in one year or in ten, that doesn't matter. The payments will be low for a ten or more year loan, even if you end up paying off the loan in one year when you re-sell the house (you should make sure there is no penalty for early repayment of the loan, which would be another aspect of the terms). These principles are true whether you are purchasing the property with a business or mortgage loan. The longer the terms, the better.

If possible, consider an interest-only loan. Even though the total interest you pay is higher, due to paying it on a higher balance, in real terms you are not paying more than if you paid some principal as well. In fact, you will be paying less over all, because interest is totally tax deductible, while your house is appreciating all the time (compounded annually) and at the same time the balance you owe (that you are paying the interest on) stays the same. If you pay 5% interest per year, and yet the house appreciates at 7% per year, this is a good deal for you. On top of that, you are upgrading the house, so it will be worth even more.

Regardless of what the other terms are, you will probably have to offer them a down payment of between 5 and 20% to secure a loan. You need to know that when making a deal, banks don't want "ifs," "buts" and "maybes". Because of this, after you negotiate and come to an agreement on all matters, you need to follow through and stick with your verbal agreement. If you don't, they'll likely never do business with you again and probably will give you a bad reputation. And so your offer, once negotiated, needs to be firm; do not change it later.

In the end, if the terms and deal are not conducive to your making any money (in other words, you know that the bank wants too much for you to pay) then you don't want it and should walk away. What is the point of doing a deal that you cannot win? It's always important to make sure you can make a profit, and a good one too. Then if things end up going wrong later, the extra profit you expected will act as a cushion.

Contractors' fees: When I was finally able to buy the house, I immediately began organizing the work that needed to be done, bringing in carpenters, plumbers, and others. I originally calculated a maximum cost for the work at $25,000. I asked the various contractors for a firm (not estimated) cost for each of their contracts in order to make sure that there would be no surprises later. Negotiating with contractors can be hazardous if you allow them to make an estimate. I have yet to find any contractor who gives an estimate and charges less than expected. Negotiating a fixed price may seem to be more money than you expected, yet it's nice not to have any surprises when the bill is finally presented. When negotiating a firm price for work by a contractor, one can always say "no" if it is beyond your budget, then look for another contractor's firm quote. Generally you will be able to get the price within your budget by going about it in this way. It should be a win-win situation, because if you cheat the contractor they will likely cheat you back in some way. All final agreements should be in writing. Open-ended verbal agreements should be avoided because there may be disagreements at the end. It is important that both sign off on what needs to be done and what is expected. Contractors are generally nice people to deal with, but they can make mistakes sometimes, and you should never be made to pay for their mistakes.

In addition to getting firm quotes from contractors and figuring all my expenses, I add an additional 12% on top of that as a contingency factor to allow for the inevitable unexpected occurrences. In this case, halfway through the work being done, the plumber advised me that he had found a major problem with the hot water boiler. He said that his cost to repair it would be close to buying a new boiler. He was honest in this regard, as he could have charged me for the repair without giving me the choice. This unexpected cost, together with some other unbudgeted expenses, added about 10% to my original calculation. Fortunately the 12% contingency allowance covered it and I therefore was still able to make about 25% profit on my total costs for all of the work and expenses in purchasing the property. All's well that ends well!

Auctions and liquidation sales

Among all your bargaining skills, it is important to keep in mind what your end result will be if you are successful. For what purpose are you buying it? For example, it may be that you have heard of a forth-coming liquidation sale of someone's home contents. Unless you are a dealer in books, furniture and carpets, etc., why should you go to a liquidation sale? Is it because you think that you might pick up a bargain? This would not normally happen. It is more common that you will get into the fever of the bidding and bid on something that you do not need or have no intention of using. If you do this, you will accumulate a lot of junk—although it can be fun doing so.

That is why it is important that you only bid on something that you really are interested in. Remember that at any auction there will normally be a number of dealers who are experts in their own sphere. For example, there will be dealers in rare books, antique dealers, and other specialized people who know what they want and how much they can resell the items for. Then there will be the second-hand dealers who are there to pick up the pieces for their own second-hand shops. And do you want to compete with them all? That would not be a good idea. You will find that the trouble is just not worth the result. Going to an auction can be fun, but just keep it at that and don't be sucked into bidding just for the sake of bidding.

I remember going to an auction once many years ago in Tasmania when a fairly new building was to be demolished to make way for the building of a bank. I was interested in getting some copper pipe for my business. The auction started in an upstairs room then moved into the main bathroom. First the toilet was auctioned, then the hand basins, then the bath, then the flooring, then the shower and fittings, all of which had to be ripped out. Finally there was the shower curtain. Someone bid one dollar, then another person bid two dollars, and then, in quick succession, several people bid aggressively so that the hectic bidding reached $14, more than twice the cost of a new one! Each bidder could just not be out-bid by another; the bidders had caught that bidding fever. At this stage, the auctioneer cut across the bidding and reminded everyone that it was only the curtain that

was being auctioned off. So much for going to auctions for the fun of it. I found the whole thing very amusing. At least I did get my copper pipe.

My recommendation to you is to avoid these types of auctions unless there is something specific you want. To go thinking that you "might find something that you want" is impulse buying, and not the right way to go about it. It would be better to conserve your funds for something better at a later date.

Negotiating overseas

When shopping overseas, it seems that everyone expects to pick up some items that are not available at home or are much less expensive. Usually it is some sort of gift item for a family member or friend. I too usually buy something when I am abroad. The important thing to recognize when overseas is that almost everyone, at least in small, privately run shops, expects you to barter—that is, haggle—over the asking price. The interesting thing is, often the sellers respect you more if you do, even if they do not show it at the time.

This was one of the rather surprising things about negotiation that I found out when I was living in Hong Kong in 1949. I found that being offered a product for a certain sum was the first test of how good a person they thought me. If I made no attempt to negotiate for a lower price, I was not thought well of. When buying general merchandise either in a store at a marked price or simply on the street, I got into the habit of dividing the asking price by three, then offering that one-third price as an opening gambit. If the opening price was, say, 10 Hong Kong dollars, I would say that I could only afford $3. The seller might reply, "No, no, I am a poor man. My family needs the money, I cannot sell it at that price. This cost me $9, but I will sell it to you for $9 because I like you. I cannot sell it at a loss." "OK, I would say, then I will give you $4, for that is as much as I can pay today." "Oh! Sir, I will take a loss and sell it to you for $8 because

I like you and you can tell your friends about me, then I can sell them something and perhaps make some profit by the extra number that I could sell." "No, my final offer is $4.50, sorry I must go now." I would then turn away as if to walk off, and I would have, but I was always stopped and allowed to purchase the item for, in this case, $4.50, usually with a big smile and a request that I should tell my friends.

When I was in Hong Kong 10 years later, I was interested in purchasing a diamond ring as a replacement one for my wife. I needed some time to choose and therefore was looking for a suitable shop that had a range of what I was looking for, yet was not full of customers. I remember how pleased the shop owner was to see me walk in. He offered me a drink of Coca-Cola and proceeded to bring out several trays of diamond rings. I instantly saw the one that I would like to buy, however I was not about to let him know this. I quickly looked over two other rings. He made several attempts to sell me a ring, giving me the prices of most of them, including the one that I wanted, for $750. But I did not bite; I was waiting to see how much lower I could get it for. He kept on talking and showing me the various rings that he had. I did not start negotiating, because it would have fixed what I wanted. I was in his shop for probably at least an hour, talking about various things. We went over his offerings several times, and each time his prices became lower and lower.

After going through them for the fourth or fifth time, the one that I was interested in was offered this time for $300. I said that I thought that the ring was quite nice and that if I could not find one that I really liked that I might come back; however, if he would take $275 for this particular ring, then I would purchase it right now. He looked at me and said, and I kid you not: "I really like you and I have had such a very good time with you during the past hour that I will let you have it for $275! However, as I will make a loss, I want you to take these cards of mine and tell your friends about me and the wonderful bargains that are available from me."

So when negotiating in overseas countries, in order to come up with the right price the formula I would recommend in general is to divide the offered price by three and multiply by two. You might ultimately settle for a little more. A more aggressive way would be to offer half of what is being asked, then settling for a figure between that price and two thirds. With these lower priced items, I always give the impression that I like the item, but feel that it is just a little beyond my pocket. I might say, "That's really lovely, but a little out of my price range." In this way I am able to get a better deal. I am still careful not to show too much enthusiasm. I find that it can be fun to haggle over prices. But even vendors need to be recompensed for their work efforts, so don't be too hard on them.

In reality, there are a great number of vendors competing for purchasing customers like you. They have already adjusted their prices to take into account negotiating offers from those wishing to buy. When you come along and make a ridiculously low offer, they will negotiate and then "reluctantly" give in and sell you the item. Both of you are pleased—you because you think that you now have a bargain and the vendor because they received above their base price.

If you simply pay the asking price, the sellers will recognize you as a sucker, or someone they can take advantage of and you are likely to be offered a "special" price that is well above what it should be, but in the process the seller will think less of you. You have not played the game of give and take that the seller expects and even enjoys.

Conclusion

Do not be embarrassed to negotiate. Outside Europe and the USA, it is fine, even expected, that negotiations will take place on almost anything. In the USA, this is still true with large sales, with big businesses, and in the sale of cars and houses. Why should anyone be ashamed to get a better price? Making our money go further is surely a worthwhile activity. It allows us to get more of the things within the budgets we have allotted ourselves. Most of us work hard to get the money we have, so why not use it to the best advantage whether we are at work or at play? If you think that bargaining and haggling for a better price is beneath you, then I can assure you that you will end up the poorer. This could translate into many thousands of dollars in a lifetime. If you don't bargain, you are giving your money away. What is the sense in that?

CHAPTER FIVE

Starting a Business: How to Do So While Avoiding the Pitfalls

It seems to me that most people, at some point in their lives, wish to start a business of some kind. I suppose that is because many of us want to be independent rather than having others tell us what to do. However, starting a successful business is no piece of cake; you can help your success by starting early.

It is rare to find young people who have become highly successful with their first business. The truth is that most successful enterprises are started by people after the age of thirty. So why do I advise starting early? The answer to this question is simple: real-world experience. When a person has a great deal of real-world experience they are much more likely to be successful than those without that experience. Statistically speaking, most first businesses fail, but the key to success in any enterprise is persevering and learning from one's mistakes; turning failures around so that, eventually, they lead to success. Even a small mistake which seems of little or no consequence at the time can turn out to have good applications later in a larger business enterprise.

One way to get some real-world experience would be by running a small sideline business while you hold a regular job or are gaining an education. What you learn will become a good foundation for your later efforts at running a larger business. It is inevitable that when we first begin, we will make wrong choices. However, the more we press on, the more experience we will gain until we are so experienced we cannot help but be successful!

In this chapter I cover principles that I have learned through a lifetime of starting businesses. There are certain principles involved that must be understood before success can be achieved, and that you will inevitably learn as you start your own business. Though nothing takes the place of real-world experience, my hope is that my sharing of these principles will jumpstart you to success.

My very first business enterprise

At the young age of seven, during the depression years of the 1930s, I discovered I could collect kindling wood for older people at the Lewisham market in London, England and be paid 3 pence for each load. Oh, how I enjoyed the money that I earned from that! Why, 3 pence would get me into a Saturday morning cinema and leave enough over for a bag of sweets or an ice cream! My normal weekly allowance from my father was half a penny. My parents had to be very frugal in what they gave away or spent. It was, after all, the middle of the depression and they had more important things to do than to spoil their children.

When I was thirteen years of age, I determined to start my own little business to get extra money for myself. Having seen a string bag made with a crochet hook, I invested in a hook and a ball of string and started to experiment with how I could make a shopping bag. I made large and small string bags with different styles of handles. I even dyed some balls of string different colors so that I could make them more attractive. I worked out that I could make a certain sized string bag in a particular amount of time; this information, combined with the cost of the materials, gave me an idea as to how much I should charge for each of them. I thought that if I paid for the materials and added a modest hourly rate for the time it took me to make them, then I could make a nice little business for myself. But in my figures I did not take into account any payment for my time to go around selling the bags or any amount to cover loss of materials such as the time when two of my bags got wet in a rainstorm and the colors ran. These days I know to cover such occurrences with an overhead and a contingency allowance, but I didn't know at the time that such a thing was necessary, never having had the experience of operating a business before.

My next hurdle was to find buyers for my bags. I did not think that advertising would be much use because it would cost me some money in advance, money that I did not have. Even if advertising had been possible, I could not be sure that I could make the hundreds of orders for bags that might come my way. So the only way that I knew to promote my business at that tender young age was to go door to door.

I was quite surprised and pleased that this approach was instantly successful, so much so that after selling my limited stock it was necessary to take orders for future bags. You can imagine the workload that I suddenly had on my shoulders! I had a standard size, but here I was being asked if I could make a different size, even a different shape, with specific colors. I remember that I had a request for a bag with two pockets. Suddenly I had to come up with a price for these newly requested one-off shopping bags, by estimating the additional materials I needed and the extra time it would take to make them. Of course, the price at which I was selling them was very attractive to my customers; my string bags were a bargain, in fact, because the price didn't include the aforementioned additional costs. It was certainly a good thing that I did not have all of the normal expenses that are usually associated with running a business, such as rent, power, telephone, motor vehicle, interest payments, wastage, and a host of other costs and financial outgoings. No substantial business could have survived under the methods that I employed. However, I was able to learn from my early mistakes without suffering any major financial setback. It was a valuable lesson for me to have the experience of starting my own little business at the tender age of thirteen.

Later I found that I just did not have enough time to make more string bags, especially as I was required to leave school and go out to work. (In England at the time, school education finished at age fourteen.) So much for my youthful endeavors! However, I did not let any of my customers go without fulfilling their orders, which was an essential part of my personal ethics. How could I not fulfill the orders that I had accepted from my nice neighbors? My honor was at stake!

So at age fourteen I started work in an office environment, where there were lots of young girls who wanted brooches, earrings, and necklaces. My next small business venture revolved around making various types of earrings and brooches for these girls. I bought the necessary tools, consisting of two pairs of pliers, a spool of silvered wire, and quite a number of beads, buttons, and metal inserts of various colors and shapes. Each one of the earrings and brooches I made was different and was readily snapped up by the girls, generally for two and six pence each. I learned quickly that the girls did not want to buy anything that was a duplicate of another. Fortunately, each set of earrings or brooches had almost unlimited computations of shape, size, and color, which meant that I could always have each of my samples different.

Here again, I only charged for my own time and materials so that my profits were still quite limited in real terms. However, in this enterprise I learned to buy only the product that I needed and at the most advantageous prices. I also learned that, as a rule of thumb, if I could sell at double the cost of my materials then I could make a nice little income. On top of this I was learning some handicraft skills. I had a steady clientele so that it was a successful small business that I could just manage in my spare time in the evenings.

About this time I realized that if I were to be able to start my own stand-alone business, I would need capital. The idea of borrowing the money did not occur to me; I doubt that I could have gotten a loan anyway. However, it did occur to me that if I wanted to start my own business one of the things I needed to do was save. And so, over time, I saved and saved until the day came that I finally did have enough money to start my own stand-alone business, and did just that. But my learning days were far from over. With my first new business I proceeded to make the mistakes that most people make when they start. However, my mistakes were all part of my eventual success.

Personal principles for running a successful business

1. Do what you love. If you want your own business, it is very important to feel good about the type of business you are starting— that is, you should like the idea of that particular enterprise, not just the idea of making lots of money. This principle may sound simple, but it is crucial. You must always start a business you are enthused about. If you have a particular interest in cooking, it would be reasonable to consider a restaurant business; if you have an outdoors interest, perhaps something to do with growing and selling produce, or even some enterprise selling hiking equipment or leading outdoor activities. The range of possibilities is enormous! Each are worthy of consideration and likely to be successful, but only if you are enthusiastic about them. It would be no good starting a fish-importing business if you did not like the smell of fish. Getting into a business that you are not interested in just for the sake of making money is a recipe for failure. This is because in such a case you will not have the enthusiasm you will need to carry you through the inevitable tough times and on to ultimate success—you will not have the staying power.

Now, what to do if you have an interest in an area but do not have a lot of firsthand experience with it yet? In this case, there are some important steps you should take. First, you should study in great detail the ins and outs of the business to get a better idea of what it involves. Be prepared to sacrifice your time to learn as much as you can about the business. Second, get practical experience by working with someone who is already in the business and who can show you the ropes. Then you will get a better idea if this is really something you want to pursue. Third, you should meet others in the workplace, again to get a better idea of the type of work involved and even to give you a better idea of how future employees should be managed. By doing these things, you will make yourself more likely to succeed in your new enterprise. I employed all the foregoing steps in my first major business enterprise—that of a mushroom farm—and it benefited me greatly.

2. Be persistent. Historically, most businesses fail within the first five to ten years after they start up. This is important to recognize so you are aware of the risks. The excitement of starting a business is no recompense to the agony of failure later, accompanied with the loss of so much money and effort. However, keep in mind that there are many examples of people who have started a business, failed, then started another and gone on to become successful, largely thanks to lessons they learned from their first failure. Failing several times might be necessary before you ultimately succeed. It is reported that Walt Disney only succeeded at starting Walt Disney Corporation after he had failed three or four times. Bill Gates failed at least once. Remember that failure is not permanent unless we never get back up and try once again. Persistence pays off.

3. Work hard. To be successful at starting your own business you must be able to work hard. If you cannot do that there is no possibility to succeed! Hard work is the lifeblood of a successful business. If you think that once you have your own business you can tell others what to do and be foot loose and fancy free, you are mistaken. Being the boss can be, and usually is, very demanding. To succeed you will likely have to work harder and longer than anyone else in the business.

You need to know everything about your business and then some. Once a sewer pipe broke on one of my mushroom farms. None of my employees knew how to mend it, and so the responsibility fell to me. After all, I was the boss! Luckily, I had done it before when working on building my first home in England, when I had had an expert to show me how. Because I knew how to do it, I was able to be the master of the situation and it was the ability to deal with many small instances like these that helped me to be ultimately successful.

4. Be willing to make personal sacrifices for the business. Making sacrifices is often necessary when starting a business and attempting to get it on a sound footing. It is a common thing to find the owners of new successful start-up companies working long hours, longer than anyone else, and even paying themselves less than the workers they employ. The owners often do not particularly care about taking money out of the business from the start because they are more interested in making the business succeed. They are quite content to receive minimum wages with no overtime pay while those who are employed receive all the advantages of overtime, holiday pay and other benefits. This is the type of mindset you need: be willing to make personal sacrifices for the furtherance and ultimate success of your business. Without this mindset you will not have what it takes to succeed when your company falls into the inevitable rough spots that will come in the future. The person who cares most about the business and is willing to do the most for it should be you.

5. Learn from your mistakes. When running a successful business you must be able to learn from your mistakes. If you are not able to correct the mistakes you will inevitably make, you will never be able to move the business in the right direction. When you make a mistake, don't be hard on yourself—live, learn, and move on.

6. **Persevere.** Perseverance is essential to success. To persevere is to keep going, even under difficult conditions. By persevering you will be able to turn your mistakes into ultimate successes. You will be able to consistently apply what you learn from your past mistakes towards not making the same mistakes in the future. Every time you pick yourself up from a wrong turn and keep going you make it that much more likely that you will ultimately succeed.

Now, all this does not mean that you should go ahead when there is really no hope, when the situation is truly doomed to fail. It is always better to save what you have now in order to be better prepared for the future rather than to continue with a company that is certain to fail and dig yourself into a bigger hole in the process. However, to give up only because you cannot take the hassle any longer is not the right approach and will not lead you to success.

7. Stay in charge. Trying to start and run a business without staying in charge is like the captain of a ship passing his responsibilities on to one of the crewmembers and then going into a port of call. The owner of the business has a responsibility to be always aware of what is going on. To give up that responsibility to another in any business is just asking for trouble. Even if the business seems to be running well without you, there is likely a time bomb ticking away and a real chance of it exploding at the wrong time!

There are many occasions when I have seen people lose charge of their business with disastrous consequences. For example, I once knew of a lady who started a McDonald's franchise with her husband. Both the husband and wife were very skilled at running their business, and eventually it grew into three franchises. Because of their success they employed an individual manager for each franchise and a supervising manager for the overall business. When the husband died unexpectedly, the supervising manager became romantically attached to the widow and eventually they were married. She, the widow, then let her new husband have full control of the total business. She did not even check up on her husband's business dealings. As it turns out, he was siphoning off much of the profits by borrowing money against the security of the whole business and putting it into real estate in his own name. Eventually the house of cards collapsed and this lady, who knew the business backwards and forwards, found herself with a mountain of debt and very few assets. And she had allowed it to happen through complete trust and zero supervision.

It is fine to have trust but it should not be without some form of supervision and questioning from time to time. If the person whom you have trusted objects to some of your probing questions, watch out! There are people in the world who seek to succeed at the expense of other people's bank accounts. They lack any loyalty to others, only to themselves! I have written extensively about these people in the chapter on scams.

8. Delegate. Although you want to stay in charge overall, it is important to be able to let go of some duties and let others do some of the work. Not to do so will create unnecessary stress. I knew of a very hard-working person who built a small successful business and then expanded it into a larger one in the same town. Eventually he built a large supermarket. But despite all his success, he could not let go of the management of all the details, and he worked very long hours. I would see him sweeping floors, packing shelves with products, and doing many of the jobs that an unskilled employee could have done. I told him that he should delegate some of his work to others, even family members. "No," he said. "If I were to leave even for a week the whole place would be in a shambles and I would lose money. There is no one that I could get to do what I do." This person literally worked himself to death. He died of a heart attack. After his death, his family, some of whom had been employed doing somewhat menial work, took over the business and ran it very well indeed. No doubt they made some learning mistakes, but that is normal. Intelligent delegating should be practiced on a regular basis, and you should allow those persons responsible to make small mistakes of their own to increase experience in your company.

9. Take a break at times. It is important to be able to take breaks from your business to re-center and refocus. "All work and no play" is not to your personal benefit in the long term! Business owners who cannot leave their business to take a break or go on a restful vacation are foolish, and they may have forgotten the aims for which they originally started the business.

Back to the previous story, the person who could not delegate also could not take breaks. When he died, he left a small fortune, yet never reaped any of the rewards of that fortune. He had lost sight of why he started a business in the first place—to create a better life for him and his family. Take time to have a break from your business, even if it means getting expensive assistance during your absence. One example of intelligent break taking is in pharmacies, where substitute pharmacists are brought in several times a year to allow the regular pharmacists to vacation. This is done to relieve the stress that builds up in that specialized business. Taking a break is important, so don't skip it.

If you are the entrepreneurial type, one way you could incorporate breaks into your life would be to sell whatever business you are currently working on once it is successful and then take a nice long rest, after which you start up another business. Restaurants and small retail businesses lend themselves to the foregoing.

As a final note, although you should always delegate and take breaks, please remember my warning. You should not leave your entire affair to one person for an extended period of time without supervision, as that will very likely cause you trouble as well.

10. Balance is best. Be careful that when you have your own business you do not become married to it. Don't let it rule you. The old saying is true, that "all work and no play make Jack a dull boy." Balance your time so that you are doing more than just work—variety is more than important, it is essential. If you focus only on work or making money and ignore the rest of your life, you will lead a very empty life. To reach the end of your years and have only money to show for it means that you have failed, even if you are rich! There are countless people who have been able to make lots of money in their lives, but those who are most remembered are those really great people who made the world a better place. Remember that making money is necessary to support life, but helping others and building relationships is what makes life worth living.

11. Know when you are beaten so you can get on with your life! In a business, it is important to be able to know when there is no hope for success, so you can cut your losses and get out with enough left to continue another pursuit. We do not like to admit defeat, but sometimes we simply must. There is a saying that, "it is no good flogging a dead horse," and that certainly applies here.

So what do you do when you think there might be a problem? There are times in a business owner's life when they know that, for whatever reason, all is not well. (Senior managements of corporations have this understanding if they are performing their responsibilities correctly.) Regular assessments of how a business is doing and its long-term viability should be done at least once a year. If you have not done one before, definitely do one now. It is very helpful to create a graph that shows the increase or decrease of both income and expenses each month and therefore profit (which is income minus expenses) over the course of several years. Otherwise you are operating in the dark.

Also, a good accountant will give you an idea of the financial health of the business and should be consulted regularly, even every three months if necessary. An accountant should be a friend that you can trust. If you cannot trust him then get another. And keep in mind that a poor quality, low-cost accountant is a liability, not an asset; you will not save money in the long-term because of what you will lose in knowledge. With accountants, you often get what you pay for.

If you are steadily losing customers and sales, then a total revamping of product and a change of direction must be considered. This is quite often done in public companies. They revamp a failing product in the direction they see is necessary in order for it to become profitable. However, if that is not possible and there is a downward trend that is irreversible, then the necessary action must be taken to bail out and move on, possibly even into a new start-up that incorporates what you have learned from your past experiences and is more pointed towards success. Hanging on to a failing business, hoping for a miracle, is a recipe for a grinding and painful failure. Do not allow yourself to bleed to death financially. It is most often the best thing to cut your losses before the business gets too deeply into trouble.

A hobby of mine is inventing. In the world of inventing, inventors quite often lose all of their available cash by keeping on with their pet project when they should give it up. They put all their money into their first invention, which leaves them without enough for any future invention, because they don't want to see the first invention fail. It is often the same with those who start their own businesses. They just cannot bear to see it all go down the drain. But knowing when to get out, and getting out when there is no hope, is the sensible thing to do because it will leave you with cash left over to start again. Do it before it is too late and there really is no more financial liquidity. I have seen so many business owners carry on against all reason, only to be forced into bankruptcy and total financial failure. Don't let it be you!

On a final note, never think that just because you have to let this one business fail, you too are a failure. The fight isn't over until you don't get up off the mat. It's OK to have another try. Perseverance, as previously mentioned, is key!

12. Put protective measures into place. When running a business, it is important to put in checks and balances that will prevent you from being robbed and prevent possible employee theft; a good example would be individuals subtly "skimming" money out of the business. Unfortunately, in business we learn that we have to be less trusting of others. The saying, "Who wants enemies when you have friends like that," is especially true in business. As a business improves and gets bigger, it naturally hires more employees. Some are honest hard workers who deserve better pay and benefits as well as promotion. However, some are not so honest and may try to rob you. Measures must be put into place right at the very beginning, as soon as is practicable, in order to protect you and the business from the disaster that could take place if such underhanded dealings are not anticipated or stopped when they are found. Be careful not to wait too long to put such measures into place, because putting checks and balances in at a later time (such as security cameras) will send the wrong message to your employees and cause resentment and distrust. Standards should be set up from the beginning that minimize the opportunity for others to rob you.

As part of your protection strategy, it is vital that you do not trust any of your employees to the point of never supervising them to some degree. Employees should be regularly questioned about what is going on in their sphere of operation. Trust has some benefits for an employer but they are limited, and the trust should only go so far. I have seen many businesses fail or be severely impacted through employee fraud. Usually it is not the one big robbery, but a steady draining of money or assets. Some trust is fine, but blind trust is dangerous. Business owners have to become judges of character, both of friends and non-friends. This is sad to say but true; if we do not take protective action now, we sow the seeds for our own future disappointment.

In the end, you will not be able to stop a determined person from stealing from you, but by being vigilant and aware you will be able minimize any major detrimental results and also put yourself in the position, once the culprit is caught, to dismiss them. Do not accept apologies and regrets by the guilty party when they are discovered. Dismiss them immediately. This includes relatives, even though later you may wish to give them a second chance. Giving anyone who has done a misdeed in your business a second chance too soon will send the wrong message to them and the other staff you employ, i.e. that doing such things will not bring high penalties and swift consequences. This will make dishonest activities more attractive to those who have such leanings and create conditions that favor such an event happening again. People who rob you must pay a price that they will understand. The dismissed employee may call you a bad person for dismissing them, but follow through anyway. Their thinking is self-centered and comes from rejecting their own guilt.

13. Do not enter into a partnership. They rarely work. While it may in theory be possible to have a successful partnership, I have never personally witnessed one. The longer they last, the more the likelyhood of problems or stagnation. Two business owners managing the same business create conditions for conflict at some point even if you like and trust each other now. At some point you will both want to have your way, but those ways will be in conflict. Then what will you do? I have witnessed many painful breakups.

Another reason for not having a partnership has to do with your own motivation and drive to succeed. If you own the business yourself (or are at least the majority owner), you will have a strong incentive to be successful because the company is yours and you are in control—the buck stops with you. However, if you are in an equal partnership, you will have less motivation because half of the responsibility is assigned to another, meaning the company is not yours and yours alone to succeed or fail. Rather it is owned by two, which will make it easy to put the blame on the other if things don't go as planned, which they never do.

As for non-equal partnerships, they are generally not good either. There is just something about split shares in a company that doesn't work well. If you want the least conflict and the highest chance for success, you need to set yourself up as central owner. Then if things go wrong you only have yourself to blame, and cannot blame another.

14. Do not involve family in your business. For one thing, employing family members is likely to cause trouble for you in the long run because of how hard it is to maintain an employer/employee relationship with them. Often there is a tendency by employed family members, because of how well they know you, to be openly vocal about things they do not agree with. Yet, in truth, they will likely not be looking at the big picture and know the whole situation. All this can be very destructive to your family relationship.

At the start of my first commercial business (back in 1952), my older brother said that he would help me for three hours every morning. After hiring him, there were problems that came up immediately. If I was even five minutes late for work he would leave and go back to his home. He said to me that I should always be the first to arrive for work; when I wasn't he became offended, thinking I wasn't working hard enough. He had his own ideas as to how a business should be run, even though he had never run one. And the biggest problem was that his ideas were not based on reality, even though I tried to explain to him that my days were often very long and that I often had to work late into the evenings, delivering product to the markets at 1:00 am. Not too surprisingly his employment with me did not last very long, but fortunately we were able to part on good terms.

Another thing not to do is to borrow money from family, or any friend you wish to remain friends with. It is a true saying, "The way to lose a friend is to lend them money!" People who want to borrow money from their family or friends often find it easy to do so, yet it is also easy not to pay the money back, and this leaves a bad taste and can seriously hurt the relationship. In starting a business, I never borrowed money from my family—for one thing they didn't have any. Yet I knew that in order to have a business of my own, I would need capital. That is why I enlisted in the British military for four years (two years was mandatory), because while in the service I earned good money yet had little time or opportunity to spend it, so I was able to save up a tidy sum.

I do have some experience lending money to family, and all I can say is that, when they don't pay me back, I find it difficult to remind them of the debt. Also I experience some level of resentment to the point that I would not be willing to assist them again. It has, for me, significantly hurt at least one relationship, which could have been completely avoided had I simply not lent the money in the first place.

Now I tell family and friends that I have a policy of never lending money. They understand. However, sometimes I give one of them money, telling them I do not expect its return. If they offer it back later, that is nice, but I do not expect it. In this way, the relationship with that person stays on solid ground.

Operational principles for running a successful business

1. Start the right business in the right location. It's easy to fall in love with a particular area of business and to think that you can make a profit doing it, but you must always analyze the business before starting it and critically think things through before concluding that a profit is likely. While enthusiasm helps a lot, it is no guarantee of success!

In my youth I would see people come to our street twice a year to offer to mend everything from broken knives to holes in frying pans. We called them tinkers. They would repair anything that was put before them. In later times, the repair business extended to radios, TVs, kitchen equipment, furniture and more. Yet now the market for such types of repair is much diminished. Models change so quickly and prices are so cheap that no one is motivated to get household appliances repaired anymore when for the price of repair they can get a brand new model that often has better features. Even the proverbial shoe repair business is languishing, and owners of such businesses are finding fewer and fewer customers even at competitive prices. And so we see that it would be a bad idea to start a repair business at this time, even if you loved mending things. There is simply no demand for such services, nor will the demand return any time soon. Starting a business in such an area would almost guarantee failure before you had even begun. I have time and time again seen businesses started in very specialized areas that do not look at the trend of the market and as a result ultimately fail. Do not let it happen to you!

2. Consider need. Another thing to look out for is businesses where there are unlikely to be many repeat customers, i.e., businesses where once the customers in your area have been satisfied, there are no more or not enough additional ones to keep the business alive. These types of businesses will not grow. You need to view the future realistically and analyze if there will be an increasing demand for the product that you intend to sell. If there is not a continuing amount of customers that will be buying from your business, then income from sales will inevitably drop causing profits also to fall, and yet all of your fixed overheads and expenses will stay the same. Eventually, if the trend continues, the overheads and expenses will become un-supportable, causing the business to fail altogether and forcing you to go out of business. Thus it is essential to know if you will have enough customers before you even start. Some examples of businesses that have this particular problem would include picture framers, furniture repairers, exotic plants, as well as many others. A continual flow of customers is highly important in assuring the ongoing profitability of any business.

Having a business in a mall, for example, has its distinct advantages because of the amount of customers that could catapult an otherwise potential failure into a success. Malls will allow you to maximize customer turnover.

Remember that in the end it is better to start a business and fail then not start one in the first place because of what you will learn from the experience. Just always be aware what might be in store for your future.

3. Consider your competition. Do not place your business near other businesses that are very similar or very different. In the case of having similar companies near your business, it is pretty clear why this is not a good idea: it will force you into fierce competition with the other stores for customers, to your own hardship and to the customers' benefit, and it could even cause the demise of your business.

Why you don't want to have companies that are too different near your business might be less clear, but it is also important to understand. If the different stores are not related, or are extremely different, it can turn away customers and even cause contention be-tween businesses. Take for example if you were to place a butcher shop between two fashion shops. The extreme difference between the stores would make the whole setup unappealing to both the customers and the other store owners.

So what is best? What you need are stores nearby that are different enough that they do not compete with you but similar enough that they complement your business, with your store tastefully placed within the group. As a rule of thumb, have at least ten stores between you and your next possible competition. It has been my experience that this is best in order to prevent you from being adversely affected by your competitors.

4. Consider the size and volume of your operation. Larger is not always better. It is good business sense to think about the future and the possibility of expanding your business, as so many do. But expanding is not always best. What you need to do is think hard about the idea of expansion, weighing the pros and cons, and try to predict what would happen by planning it out in detail. Successful expansion or diversification should mean more profits, yet if the expansion is not right for the business you will not profit. I distinctly remember a bright businessman whose philosophy was, "The more I sell, the more money I will make." He employed more and more sales people, advertised on local TV stations, and increased his sales tenfold. But he had not done his math or thought ahead. He did not realize that while his total income increased dramatically, his expenses increased as well. His overall expenses ended up being greater than his total income, and of course no business can survive for very long when that is the case. The business lasted for about ten months and then imploded.

The idea sometimes goes around in the business world that selling a higher volume will make up for losses, but this is false. Losses are not going to go away by simply selling more product. As we have seen, selling more may also increase your expenses—sometimes more than the added income. Selling more does *not* automatically mean higher profits.

Another aspect of expanding is the stress level it will bring on. Most businesses have the potential to become larger, which might sound great, but in the case of the individual owner, bigger seldom is better. This is because the new responsibilities on the individual will create a higher stress level. No matter how much or where they may delegate, the ultimate responsibility—and thus the most stress—will still rest with them. And personal stress is a negative in several areas. People become less efficient, more susceptible to illness, less able to think correctly and make good decisions, and more at risk of making those catastrophic decisions that can sink a business entirely. It is far better to make $1,000 per day with little stress than to make $2,000 per day with a crippling stress load. I have seen the death of many successful businessmen to heart attack, hypertension, and other illnesses because of the stress brought on by too many responsibilities. The big business life sounds great, but the reality is that it comes with many difficulties. Never forget that a good business does not have to be expanded too fast or even at all.

In addition to stress and higher expenses, expansion can lead to consequences you have not seen or contemplated beforehand. Some people have the potential for great business achievement, yet this very achievement can, if they are not careful, get to their heads. I have seen many so-called successful businessmen with failed marriages and broken homes—with the resulting financial and emotional consequences—all in the name of professional achievement! The loss of a person's family and their children's love and respect is a terrible price to pay for success. So be warned: bigger is not always better. True profits are not measured in money, assets or position, but by advancement in every level of life, including personal relationships and personal health.

5. Be familiar with supply and demand. Knowing how supply and demand works is very important to running a successful business. It will allow you to understand and properly anticipate what your business market will do.

So what is supply and demand? Essentially it is that more supply or availability of a product (or less demand) will mean that you will not be able to sell the product for as much. Conversely, more demand for a product (or less supply) will mean that you will be able to sell the product for a higher price. In my life I have never encountered any exceptions to this rule.

As an illustration, just imagine that you had the only cow and bull in the world, the only chicken and rooster, or the only sheep and ram. How much would a breeder be willing to pay you for them? It is easy to see that the price you could ask would be very high because of the high demand but low supply. However, if there were many of such animals, it is easy to see that the price of each of them would be greatly reduced because of the greater supply and consequent lesser demand.

6. "Anything that can go wrong will go wrong." People laugh at Murphy's Law, yet I have found out the hard way that it is very necessary to be aware of the potential for things to go wrong. Things will eventually go wrong (to a greater or lesser degree) in any business, no matter what you do. It is inevitable! What is important is that you are prepared. You must constantly ask yourself what might go wrong and have a plan in place to counter it. You should also personally prepare yourself so that you are not surprised when something does happen. That way you will be able to handle more calmly any problem that comes.

One event you should absolutely prepare for is sickness, whether for yourself or other employees. If you do not plan for this and it happens, you will find yourself in a bad situation because suddenly you will have to find someone to fill in or risk lower productivity and customer dissatisfaction. Facing this problem before it happens will keep you safe. There are several ways you could prepare for sickness, such as having a family member "hold the fort" and controlling the situation by phone, or by having a person you can call at a moment's notice to fill in—it all depends on the situation and the nature of your business. But without a doubt you must plan for it, as it will happen, and generally at the wrong time for you.

The truth is that in business the longer things go smoothly, the higher the chance that something important has been missed and you are heading for a setback. When things continually go well it is easy to get lulled into a sense of well-being; you become lax and it becomes easy to miss the little warning signs, which paves the road for future trouble. When something does happen, you are not prepared and are caught in a real bind. Remember that it is all about planning for the unexpected; being ready for changing circumstances is the only way you will remain successful, and this fact is true of all businesses. If you are prepared you will be able to face any problem with ease, but if you are not prepared it could cause your downfall.

7. Be aware of cash flow. Be particularly mindful of *when* you are being paid for products and services. Even if you make a lot of sales and are showing a profit, you can still increase your debt and cause your business to fail because of the all-important factor of when the money arrives. If you receive the income late, then your ability to pay your bills on time could be in jeopardy, which will make your suppliers nervous. Also if you do not pay your bills on time there will be financial penalties in one form or another. Remember that your suppliers have no interest in your profitability or in how many people owe you money, but rather that they are paid on time. After all, they have their own expenses to pay.

The solution to this problem is to have a reserve fund such as a bank line of credit that you can use strategically to pay your present expenses while waiting for your future income to arrive. I cannot stress enough how important it is to have this. I have seen so many businesses fail due to lack of control over the time when the earnings come in, because they then lack the ability to pay their expenses. A bank's line of credit helps you to make the most of your resources because it means you do not have to have cash in the bank doing nothing for long periods of time in order to cover your finances. Being able to quickly borrow sufficient operating capital for the smooth running of the business means that you will sleep more comfortably at night.

As a side note, it is vital to your business that those who do not pay within the time allotted them be charged interest. In the business world this is called a finance charge. This is necessary in order to deter people or other businesses from paying you late and also to pay you back for the troubles you incur by the delayed payment.

8. Be calm rather than aggressive. Having a relaxed attitude with everyone you meet—such as customers, associates, staff, suppliers, friends and acquaintances—pays high dividends and helps you keep focused on your real job, which is to successfully run the company and not to make other people stressed. To be firm with others is OK if necessary, but making strong, pointed, and aggressive remarks to others, in any business, is not a good thing to do if you are looking for long-term success. Losing an otherwise good staff member because you chewed them out aggressively for some minor reason is not good for business. If there really is a problem, it is best to try to put yourself in the other person's place and to sit down and talk with them to see what their reasoning was for what they did. The gentle approach is always the one you should use. This way you will avoid conflict, be able to understand the situation better, and ultimately be able to respond to the issue in question in a responsible and clearheaded way. If being aggressive is in your nature, then this is something you need to work on and correct if you wish to be successful at running a business and in dealing with people.

Financial principles for running a successful business

1. Have a forward budget for the business. Having a budget in business, just like in one's own personal life, is essential for ultimate success. Living within one's means goes the same for businesses as well as individuals. You are in business to make money, but you can't realistically expect to succeed if you do not have complete control over where your money goes or know with certainty where your income is coming from and how much it will be. How can you know where you want your business to go, yet not have a budget to get it there? Money is like fire: a good friend and a bad enemy. Without the knowledge necessary to manage money, you will get burned.

2. Always figure overheads and contingencies into your pricing. I knew of a contractor who wanted to make an 8% profit on his costs each time he built a home. In order to arrive at his final price he would work out how much the materials and labor would cost him, add a minimal overhead allowance for such things as power and water, and finally add 8% for his profit. However, it often happened that after starting, the purchaser would want just a little extra done here and there on the home which the builder was happy to do but did not charge for or account for in his figures. Neither did he figure in extra cost to cover things such as running his truck, car, or phone. He also made no allowance for contingencies—the inevitable things he could not plan for and which would end up happening. All of these things added up to the point that he almost always lost money on each home that he built. He was a master builder, but unfortunately very poor.

Any person who starts a new business has to keep a close eye on the costs to produce their product or service. They will quickly find out through experience, if they don't know already, that if they only price according to their direct costs (such as cost of materials and cost of labor) they will quickly lose money. This is because in any business there are more than just direct costs involved. Depending on the business, other costs could include selling costs, advertising costs, bank charges and interest, commissions, insurance premiums, telephone and utilities expenses, rent, and many other intangible expenses. The cost of overheads cannot be figured directly like other expenses because they are variable and hard to nail down, and so they are figured into the final pricing by way of percentage rather than being individually calculated. You always need to have some sort of overhead figured in, otherwise you will get yourself into trouble; however, even with overhead costs figured in by way of percentage, you will find through experience that this added amount is still insufficient to cover all your costs. In order to cover absolutely *all* of your costs you will learn that it is necessary to include an additional percentage on top of overhead called a contingency allowance. Contingencies are those unforeseen things that can and do happen. This would include late deliveries of supplies, a severe illness of a manager, serious delays due to weather, legal entanglements, and a host of other possibilities. Allowing for contingencies is often overlooked by businesses and is the cause of many a company's downfall.

So what is the right percentage to figure in? Overheads in any business should run between 10-20% above the estimated costs, depending on the business. The higher the expected overheads for the business the higher the percentage should be. 15% is a fair compromise when you're not sure of exactly the right figure. In order to get your overhead counted into your price, divide the total estimated cost of your materials and labor by one hundred and multiply it by one hundred and fifteen.

What is the right percentage for your contingency allowance? This is done by taking the previous total you got after factoring in the overhead allowance and then doing in essence what you did before; namely, dividing the new figure by one hundred and then multiplying it by one hundred and the contingency percentage. Always remember when calculating your price to figure in the overheads first; then afterwards use that total to next figure in your contingencies. Depending on the type of business (some of which may have higher risks associated with them) the percentage of contingency to figure in will be between 8-15%.

Finally, after figuring both overheads and contingencies, it becomes time to figure in your profit. To figure in your profit, divide the total you got after figuring in contingencies by one hundred and multiply it by one hundred and the percentage of profit you want (a good average is 15%). This final figure then becomes the correct price to sell!

Never forget that in order to get the right final price, each factor needs to be done in sequence and not all together, and it is always figured in this order: basic costs, then overheads, then contingencies, and then profits. If you lump all of the figures together it will give you an incorrect result.

It is always possible to adjust the final price of your product or service when circumstances change, but it should never be varied too much, as will become evident below. Remember, you are in business to be successful, not to make a loss. So be aware that the overheads are always there to a greater or lesser degree, and always need to be accounted for. Also, contingencies themselves may not happen right away; however, they will happen sooner or later; you can be sure about it!

3. Allow for the fact that people who are employed for a certain number of hours will not give you that many hours of work. One thing you need to be aware of when you calculate your basic labor costs is that there is more cost than just what you pay them. This is because you don't get eight hours of work when employing someone for eight hours. Breaks, coming to work, clocking in, leaving work, downtime, bathroom time, etc. all eat into that eight-hour figure. The truth is that to have someone work for eight hours strictly without ever doing anything other than work is nigh to impossible. The disparity between how much a person has been clocked in and how much work they have actually done has to be covered somehow, or you will put yourself in financial jeopardy. This can be accomplished when figuring your basic costs by allowing for nearly double the employees' hourly rate. This will also allow for the additional costs of state taxes, insurance, holiday pay, sick pay, etc. that you will have to pay each time you employ someone. All costs of employment need to be allowed for.

4. Do not overspend. The problem with overspending is that then you do not have the money to spend again. Most businesses that fail, large and small, fail because of lack of sufficient money reserves. There are times when that little extra cash will make all the difference between riding out a difficult time successfully or having to go out of business because of it. By throwing your good money away on things that are not necessary, you make it that much more likely that your money reserves will be depleted at a time when you need them. To prevent this, you need to keep a tight hold on all your spending to conserve that all-important reserve of cash. In addition, keep in mind that if you conserve your money and spend it wisely, then it will be easier to get more money. When a business is successful it is much easier to get a bank or people to invest in it and lend it money than when a business has problems. This is the case even though the business in trouble needs the extra money more than the successful one. Investors want to invest in success and not failure. By not overspending and keeping a tight hold on the money you have, it will be much more likely that you will have the necessary cash when it is really needed, that you will get the loans you need, and that your business will ultimately succeed.

5. Always cover your costs. Of course, this has to be the fundamental aim of all businesses. If there was no hope of covering your costs, then why have a business? If the money coming into a business does not at least equal the money going out, then the operation must eventually close down. You cannot operate at a loss for very long (unless the business is a government entity). This is even true of nonprofit organizations that have workers willing to donate their time for free. All volunteer organizations still have operational expenses that must be sustained, even if it is only to pay for utilities or transportation.

6. Create the right balance of profit margin and expenses. Profit margin is essentially the percentage of profit you make on what you sell. When looking at your profit margin, you don't want to see that for every dollar you sell there is a small percentage of profits and a large percentage of expenses. This is because if the profits you are making are too small, then the power you have to move your business forward is hindered. Conversely, you also do not want to see that in every dollar you sell there is a very large profit percentage and a very small percentage for expenses. This is because if the amount of profit is too big, other companies will likely come in with a lower price and take your customers away (though if you have exclusive rights to something it will allow you to have a higher profit percentage than normal). Ideally there should be a balance between the two, so that for every dollar you sell there is a reasonable percentage of profit and a reasonable percentage of expenses.

7. Do not reduce prices to try and increase profits. Profits are the bread and butter of a business. Selling goods and services at a profit is the aim of every good business owner. If the business owner thinks that by reducing the price they charge, it will result in more business, they are probably correct. However it can often backfire if the profit margin is too low. Profits can slip away from you if you are not vigilant.

You cannot usually lower your price dramatically without it seriously affecting your profit margin. Remember that basic overheads and other basic fixed costs remain the same no matter how many products you sell, so when you lower your price you naturally lower your percentage of profit as well. Also, to lower your price means that you are likely trying to increase the volume that you sell, yet more volume will inevitably mean higher labor costs because of additional staff needed, increased product processing costs, increased marketing costs, and increased variable overheads. All of these additional expenses may reduce the profit margin even more. Finally, once you reduce the profit margin it is usually very difficult to return the price to its original state, much less raise it beyond that. And so reducing prices to counter a competitor or to increase profits is generally a poor way of operating a business. Rather, you should look at your profit margin as your benchmark and try to get the biggest profit that the market will reasonably bear. In other words, being the cheapest is a recipe for failure. It is better by far to be known for charging a higher price and giving superb service and quality! Customers always want service ahead of price, and they also know that a cheap price often means cheap goods or service. Service, quality, and a somewhat higher price will almost always win out *in the long term* over bad service, poor quality, and a lower price.

On a sobering note, I was once involved peripherally with a business that sold specialized landscaping materials. The management at the top decided that they could sell twice as much material if they reduced their prices by one third. This they did, but it did not turn out as they expected. It was a case that the more they sold, the more money they lost and it culminated eighteen months later in a total meltdown of all their tangible assets. Their suppliers alone lost nearly $400,000. And so we see that the idea that reducing prices and increasing volume will automatically increase profits is not true—business just does not work that way.

8. Don't make too many sacrifices in order to keep and gain customers. What about lowering prices for the occasional customer? It will help you maintain your price if you always keep an eye on your ability to make a profit. To sacrifice profit in order to satisfy a customer is a recipe for trouble unless it's to help keep a long-standing customer—but even then it should only be a one-time thing. If a customer puts pressure on you to give them a special price that will prevent you from making a profit, you need to firmly resist. Remember that if you give in, even once, it can hurt you in additional ways because what you give to one customer, other customers will want as well. There are many customers that will try to squeeze you into a non-profit position for their own benefit, but it is of the utmost importance that you do not succumb to the pressure. If they really want you to supply them with your product, they should pay prices that will ensure that you will survive, and part of that is making a profit. Everyone wants lower prices, but if people really thought about it they would not want prices so low that it forced an otherwise great company to go out of business. Then no one would be able to have the services or products they provide. The truth is, in the end, it is much better to allow such a customer to go elsewhere and find out that you are in fact the best supplier and the one with the best service and prices. They will soon come back to you and pay the price you ask. Great service along with competitive prices will ensure that customers keep coming back. Never forget that sharpening one's pencil to give better prices to "special" customers has ruined many a business enterprise.

The importance of resisting giving a special low price is especially true in the case where a customer wants you to supply them with one third or more of your production. It can be very enticing to be asked to supply a large company with a large order, but watch out! The very large customer could very well become the essential mainstay of your operation, and then you would be in a very bad position. This is because it could get to the point that without them you cannot stay in business, and if this is the case you can easily become subject to a type of price blackmail from them. They will be able to make you do what they want, because otherwise you are finished. A large customer will not want to squeeze you so much that you go out of business and cannot supply them, but they will have enough leverage that they can force you to make very low profits, and essentially cause you to be hostage to them. I have seen this type of thing happen on many occasions. Profit margins are reduced, capital expenditures are increased, overheads rise, and sale prices go down—all in order to be able to supply the big customer, but at the same time playing havoc with your business. As said, this is a very bad position to be in.

In addition, there are other reasons why I have always felt that it is unwise to "put all your eggs in one basket" and let one company become your main customer. Besides opening you up to possible blackmail, it opens doors to other unfortunate possibilities. For example, if you are dependent on a large customer and they get into trouble, you will be in trouble too because they are your main source of revenue.

9. Increase your prices each year to keep up with true inflation. This very important and very necessary thing needs to be done annually if a business, large or small, is to survive over the long term. You must increase the price of all the items in stock each year by at least the rate of inflation from the previous year (and by inflation I mean the true inflation rate, not the official government rate). If this is not done consistently, and on an annual basis, it will cause the business eventually to have to close down and could even cause you to go bankrupt. Often, businesses go under because they fail to keep pace with inflation. They do not realize that keeping prices the same from year to year will cause their eventual downfall.

When I was a young lad, there was a hardware store that I knew in the village of Biggin Hill, Kent, about twenty miles southeast of London. There were all types of hardware in stock from nails and screws of all sizes to garden and professional tools. Each had a price tag to show how much the item cost. There must have been several hundred types of items, mostly within the small to very small range. I started my first business in Biggin Hill and purchased many items from the store at what I considered to be bargain prices. You see, the selling prices of the items on display had all been marked many years previously, and had never been adjusted for inflation. The owner was a nice person, but this did not save him from having to close the business down within a few years.

There is often a general feeling that it is wrong to increase prices, yet any business is doomed if prices are not raised on a periodic basis. Of course, everyone wants to pay the least amount for services and products, yet I have found throughout my life that a steady rise occurs. Nothing stays the same! Those who keep to the old prices find that they can't pay expenses. When they finally realize they need to increase prices, the shock to their customers of such a large increase in price in a short amount of time causes the customers to go elsewhere, even if the service was good. It is far better to increase the price gradually over time. I have found that annual increases at the real inflation rate are generally accepted, but waiting two years (or more) and then increasing prices at double the rate of inflation (or more) is generally not accepted without some grumbling or loss of customers. Better a little and often than a large amount less often.

Whatever you do, do not reduce prices. I have found that to reduce prices, except for clearance stock or unwanted items, ends up creating serious problems. Once the normal previously established prices are lowered, raising them again later, even just to what they were before, becomes very difficult because of the strife from customers. Of course when raising prices, if productivity has improved, prices may not need to be increased so much. Then to inform your customers that there will be no increases for, say, eighteen months, creates loyalty and good will from them. And when you do increase prices, it becomes possible for you to then strategically give discounts to certain regular, good paying customers.

So what is the true inflation rate that should be used? I estimate the present actual inflation to be around 7.2% compounded annually, or approximately the doubling of prices every ten years. As I have said in the chapter on Money and Inflation, the lower government figures are not correct because they do not take into account the price of staples along with the price of many other goods and services such as taxes.

10. Keep a tight hold on your basic inventory and the finances associated with them. Keeping control of inventory so that there is neither too much nor too little but rather just the right amount (sufficient for the operating needs, with some appropriate cushioning for safety) is essential. Basically, you want to have enough inventory to cover your normal anticipated sales for 30 days. You do not need more than this. Yes, it is true, you may not have all that you need for an emergency order, but that is OK, because if you did have enough to cover an emergency order, it would increase the capital tied up in inventory, and having your financial resources tied up in inventory is seldom a good idea. You want to make your money work for you, not against you, and when your money is tied up in inventory it is not working for you because it is not doing anything. The money could be better put to use elsewhere. The truth is that it is not desirable to have a contingency of product in stock at any one time. Having a 30 days' supply of anticipated sales is enough, though this does depend on the type of product you are selling. 30 days gives you what a normal business is likely to sell even with increased orders. This way you will have some reserve, but not too much.

At some point you may be offered a special deal by your supplier to purchase three or even six months of supplies at a special reduced rate. Generally speaking, you should not take advantage of their offer. This is because, as said before, you do not want too much money tied up in inventory and, in addition, you would have to find storage for it, which would cost even more money. Besides, what is the reason your supplier is offering you the special deal? It must benefit them in some way. There might be a better model or other improvement that necessitates them getting rid of their surplus inventory. Do you really want to be left with their old product? It all adds up to being a better decision for you to decline their offer.

So what happens if you are asked to get a rush order to your customers? Sending your product to them more quickly will cost more than normal and your expenses will be higher, which will lower your profit margin. If a rush order is requested, the best thing to do, if you can, is to pass the extra cost onto the ordering customer by saying that you can't send it unless they pay extra. This will keep them mindful of the extra cost of not keeping their own inventory to its proper level.

11. Do not buy a business on credit. Buying a business on credit will mean more loans that have to be paid back, usually on a monthly basis, with interest that is typically higher than normal because the lender has more risk. Loading yourself down with debt right at the beginning opens the door for considerable worry later. Making a profit out of a business that you are running with the added burden of repayments can be very hard on you. All this you want to avoid, considering that starting your own business is likely to give you enough stress from other areas!

You especially need to avoid buying a business on credit from the seller. The seller will have no mercy on you if things go wrong, as they often do. Some sellers drive such a hard bargain that they fully expect to eventually foreclose and repossess their old business, pocketing all the money and value that you have put into it in the meantime. To buy a business from an owner, with a low down payment, almost always results in a foreclosure later by the seller.

Conclusion

In the end, keep in mind that if the financial rewards of starting the business you like are not considerably better than what could be received by being employed by another, then it should not be attempted. The reasons for this are that if you are employed, there is some level of security such as regular vacations, perhaps sickness insurance and weekends free from concern. You will not have to constantly be on the phone to customers that have to speak to you at all hours of the day! Make no mistake, operating a business venture is not for the faint of heart. It sounds and feels as if it could be fun and profitable, yet there are stresses and strains that are not present when you are employed by someone else.

Having your own business is not for everyone. It is important to find out if it is for you and accept the conclusion you come to. If the would-be business owner is subject to worry on a consistent basis and is anxious about failure, then they should avoid any business venture till that worry has been minimized. Worry over money in a business enterprise can be fatal for future business decisions. Minimizing worry of course does not mean that there will be no loss. Early on, at the beginning, some losses are to be expected. But to start a business with the fear of failure can be self-fulfilling!

While it's true that the great majority of businesses fail within the first ten years of operation, don't let this get you down. As I've said, and as I firmly believe, failing in a business venture is not necessarily a bad thing. If you are persistent and learn from your mistakes, such failures will certainly pave the way to ultimate success!

CHAPTER SIX

Long-term Investing: The Winning Strategy

There are many ways to invest in the stock market if you have a lot of time or are a professional market player. However, this book is not for the full time day-to-day player! With few exceptions those people generally get burnt out or cashed out, sooner or later. Rather, this chapter is on investing in the stock market long-term and from an outsider's perspective. I am not a specialist in any one investment field, but rather an independent investor who has had a whole range of interests in many of the acknowledged fields, most of which are covered in this book. Because of this, I have been able to take a broad view of the essentials for proper investing, which I would like to pass on to you.

I do not claim to know everything about the financial industry, nor do I believe that any person can know all aspects of it. It is far too complex a subject, and one that is constantly changing to suit new conditions and needs. However, I will share with you techniques that have worked for me and are grounded in real world experience. My approach in general is a psychological one. I use something I call "con-sequential thinking" to come to conclusions which others may not. Dealing with the stock market has given me the most challenges of any of my life-long investment experience, but has ultimately led to me developing a way where anyone can profit from it long term. It is also a way that is about as safe an investment as you can make.

All investments have risks. The truth is that in the *short-term*, a "safe" investment does not exist. What I mean is that any amount of money that you may invest for the short term will be totally at risk for partial or total loss no matter what you invest in. Businesses can fail, land speculation can take a long time and profits can get eaten up in taxes, interest charges, inflation and government red tape. Markets can go down as well as up. Commodities can fluctuate so as to force liquidation of your account. A host of things can go wrong, and if Murphy's Law has anything to do with it, they will! However, you can guard against it by investing wisely with your own safeguards in place, and that is what this chapter will teach you: how to invest wisely in the stock market for the *long-term*. While the financial industry is constantly changing, the strategy outlined in this chapter will not change over time because it is based on true principles. By using the following investment procedures you will be on solid ground.

The importance of investing yourself

Before we move, on, I want to address one point. It is generally thought that to be successful in investing, you need the services of an expert, or certainly one who has a good background in their area of expertise, someone who will be able to make all your investment decisions for you. The great problem for the "man in the street," of course, is picking the right person, one who will have the investor's well-being as their primary concern. There are good people out there, and many of them have vast knowledge and experience so that their advice has much merit. However, is there a less stressful, less risk-filled way to invest that is, in the long-term, more sensible? There is! And that is by doing it yourself.

As a long-term investor, you are looking for long-term results of more than fifteen years. You cannot expect that the same individual is going to handle your account all this time, no matter how great an advisor he is. When your investments are controlled by others, the people behind your investments might die, change jobs, pass your investment management to someone else (probably for a fee), swindle you, or do any one of a dozen other things. I have seen such things happen many times. But all of this can be avoided by handling your investments yourself. The rest of this chapter will aid you in doing just that.

How the market works

The market in publicly traded shares is fundamentally the same as markets have been over the past six thousand years or so: there is a buyer and a seller who must come to an agreement, otherwise no sale is possible. This is true if you are selling a house, land, kittens, or potatoes. Each side has to agree on the exchange terms. In any market there are market factors that will move a particular stock up or down, mostly supply and demand. If there are more buyers than sellers for a particular stock, then the price of that stock will tend to move upward. If on the other hand there are more sellers than buyers, then the price of the stock will naturally move downward. Sometimes it is a daily thing, sometimes a weekly thing, sometimes monthly or longer. But movement up and down in the price of stocks is normal.

The stock market is also driven by news—good news and bad news—that comes in from all over the world. The news could be of floods or drought, wars or rumors of wars, etc. On the home front, the news of a large company reporting good (or bad) earnings will create an effect on the prices of other stocks, especially in related fields. Stocks will also move up or down on sentiment: the weather, the price of commodities, the report of some government or private agency, what someone has said, and so on. All this and more have the end effect of moving the various stocks (and the whole market) up or down.

In an upward trending market (called a "bull market"), the market does not go straight up, but rather two steps forward and one step backwards, with higher highs and higher lows, just like climbing a ladder and taking a step back every once in a while, or like trekking up and down mountains with the mountains getting progressively higher. There is always a periodic retrenchment of the stock market and/or an individual stock. You, the share purchaser, can take advantage of this by looking at the recent chart and placing a buy order in a trough and thus buying at a more advantageous price.

When the price of a stock reaches a certain height it will usually fall back, or retrench, often to consolidate the price before going higher. A ten percent retrenchment from a recent high is quite common, fifteen percent less common, and over twenty percent rare. A twenty percent retrenchment for any company would indicate something radically amiss, either in the stock or the market as a whole. This happened during the financial market turndown during late 2007 and into 2008. The whole sector was severely beaten up, and even the companies that were not exposed to the major retrenchment, tended to come down in sympathy.

For the stock market as a whole to retrace 15% or more indicates a "bear market." A bear market is a down trending market, when stocks in general go more and more down in a pattern of lower lows and lower highs—just the opposite of a bull market. How long a bear market will last depends on a number things, such as the state of the economy, the unemployment rate, the interest rate (which has the biggest effect), the price of property, and world sentiments, but on average a bear market will generally last for up to a year before it ceases to go down and gradually begins to turn around. Notwithstanding a bear market, the high-worth stocks (the ones *you* will be investing in) generally hold up well, and do better than the cheaper, more speculative stocks. You lose nothing in a bear market unless you panic and sell, because the companies in which you own stock still pay dividends.

No one likes to see their particular stock go down, yet this is an inevitable occurrence with every stock. It is the long-term trend that has to be considered. If it is a good stock that produces needed articles or services, then a downward bias is an opportunity to purchase more stock at a lower price. It is certainly not a time to worry or even think of selling. Far from it! As you will learn, if you are in the market for the long haul (at least five years), retrenchments can be a benefit to you. Be prepared for such occurrences so that you can take advantage of them by buying more shares at the temporarily deflated price.

More on the various markets

In the United States the stock market is made up of two main *exchanges* called the National Association of Securities Dealers

Automated Quotations (NASDAQ) and the New York Stock Exchange (NYSE). The function of these two exchanges is to transfer ownership of the various stocks that are listed with them. Each exchange has requirements in order for a company to be listed on their particular exchange. In addition to the exchanges, there are also several sub markets that are part of the larger exchange markets.

In the stock market there are also various arbitrary *indexes* that have been created in order to track the performance of certain groups of stocks. Indexes are quite separate from the stock exchanges themselves, and serve as benchmarks for the stock market as a whole. The most well-known of these indexes are the Dow Jones Industrial Average (DJIA), the Standard and Poor's 500 (S&P 500), and the Russell 2000.

The Dow Jones Industrial Average is composed of the thirty highest-valued US stocks (by capital worth). The number of the DJIA is the average of all the prices of those 30 stocks at any one time. It is a very prestigious group of stocks and an important number to keep an eye on to see the trends in the market, up or down. The number is constantly on the move.

The S&P 500 is a group of 500 companies that represent the top 500 US stocks (by capital worth and covering a broad range of industries). It is divided into ten segments which cover all of the main types of business in the USA. Some of these businesses would be from the NASDAQ and some from the New York Stock Exchange. In the S&P 500 are the big names of the world of business. These companies only remain in the S&P so long as they meet certain criteria which, as mentioned before, is connected with the overall capital value of their stock (which is the number of shares outstanding multiplied by the average price of the stock).

The Russell 2000 is an index that tracks 2000 *smaller* capitalized companies. Each of these companies generally aims to get into a broader, more prestigious market when they become more successful and their shares command a higher price.

New groups and indexes are being invented all the time, and they are very hard to keep up with. As a long-term investor you need not worry about them. These indexes are traded by speculators of all varieties who try to buy and sell them to their advantage, just like buying and selling mutual funds, yet it is a kind of gambling speculation which you should not participate in. You should only be interested in owning stocks that appreciate in value and can pay out good dividends.

Mutual funds

Also in the stock market is something called a mutual fund, which is in essence a fund that buys, sells, and holds stocks and other financial instruments such as municipal and corporate bonds. Mutual Fund organizations receive money from investors and then buy stocks they think will go up in price (and sometimes they sell stocks they think will go down—called "selling short"). They have the advantage in that they can cover a wide range of stocks so that the risks associated with buying one stock and seeing it go down are minimized.

At the time of writing there are over 8,000 mutual funds, and the number is constantly going up (even though some go out of business) due in part to the money to be made by their various promoters. Their share portfolios have within them different combinations of stocks, depending on what their main aim is, whether it be aggressive, conservative, environmental, financial, or a host of others too many to enumerate. For the individual, long-term investor, it is a minefield to figure out which mutual fund would be the best to invest in, and any advice to buy would only be the personal preference of the advisor.

Despite their popularity, I do not consider mutual funds to be a good long-term investment for several reasons. For one thing, and this is important, they do not appreciate on a net return basis as much as annual inflation. Even though they may hold certain stocks that do appreciate with (or more than) inflation, all their operational expenses have the effect of canceling out that increase. Mutual funds have a layer of expenses on top of the expenses of the stocks themselves, including office costs, salaries for their professional, well-paid staff, directors' fees, and commissions to key personnel. It is what you could call "double jeopardy," doubling up on expenses. The mutual fund is acting like the owner of the stocks, just as if you owned them, but unlike if you owned them, they cannot compound their gains because they usually only buy and sell short-term and also by law they have to declare to the IRS any gains or losses they have at the end of the year which has tax consequences for the mutual fund itself and *in addition* has tax consequences for you, the owner of the mutual fund shares. As a whole mutual funds are a poor performer—out of 8,000, there are very few that outperform the market. But even with the few that do outperform, past performance is no guarantee of future success. The nature of mutual funds in general makes such guarantees impossible. I'll cover a little more on why that is later.

Dividends

Dividends are another important thing to consider when dealing with the stock market. A dividend is a payout of some of the profits earned by a company to the shareholders of that company. It is paid out in order to keep shareholders contented and loyal. Unless a company is a growing one that puts all of their profits into their expansion projects, they will usually pay a portion of their profits to their shareholders by way of dividends.

Interestingly enough, when the price of a stock goes lower, the percentage of return to the holders of those shares (by way of dividend) will usually be higher because the dividend payout normally stays the same. For example, if you were to buy a quality stock for $50 and it is paying a 2% dividend, which equals $1 per share per year, and if, during a severe downturn in the market. the share price were to go down to $25, you would still normally get a $1 dividend, which would now be the equivalent of a 4% return. Not a bad return for your investment! This is because the company pays dividends based on what they earn—how much profit they make—rather than what the price of their share is at any given moment.

Analysts, advisers, and account executives

In the stock market there are professionals who are steeped in its day-to-day operations. Three of these people who are important to know about are analysts, financial advisers, and account executives.

Analysts: Analysts either work for a stockbroker or for themselves and become an "expert" in dealing with the various companies. They examine company news (that is, news given out by the various companies) and naturally also go to the various annual shareholders' meetings as well as any appropriate shows that the company may be involved with. Generally they have an inside track to the latest news, which they distribute to their clients. They often recommend a rating on the stocks that they cover, such as *Buy, Hold,* or *Sell.* These analysts often have a price target for the shares they are covering, which is their prediction of where they believe the price of the stock will go. It turns out that the price of shares is often influenced by what analysts say. Even so, two analysts might see the stock differently and take different, even opposing views.

Financial advisers: Advisers make a living advising others on how to invest their money. They have often obtained a degree in business management, and usually cover a limited number of investments, not the whole spectrum of the market. Often they get their income from a percentage of what you are investing and may also charge consulting fees. If the amount to be invested is small, they might charge a flat fee for their work.

Usually advisers are very conservative in their investment strategies and stress their idea of the safest way to invest your money. This is because they do not want to make mistakes. They will also make it plain to you that they cannot guarantee a good end result in any advice given. Advisers are mindful of the possibility of legal action against them or the companies that they work for, should their advice be wrong. I have no quarrel with advisers, they have a necessary function. Some are very good at what they do. Unfortunately, too many are much too conservative. Conservative means trying to be safe, and yet when you try to be safe you tend to invest in things that are guaranteed to lose value because of inflation, and not to invest in other things that are in fact good opportunities. Therefore, you lose out. The real truth is that there are no truly "safe" investments. They don't exist. However, the good news is that coming from the angle of keeping the true value of, and even increasing, your money, the procedures outlined in this chapter are as safe as they come.

As an aside, should you consult a professional adviser? The answer is, if you can manage your own account from time to time, no, because the benefits of doing it yourself outweigh that of having a professional adviser. However, if you cannot manage it yourself, and still want to invest, then yes. They can take the edge off your work load, but even so, do not expect stellar performance. If they were truly great investors they would soon be out of the advising business and into their own portfolios. Also, check their background. Many simply rely on the advice of others and little else. Not all advisers are equal. Many have very little firsthand experience in the marketplace. Finally, remember that advisers need paying! The more they do for you, the higher the service fee that will be charged.

Account executives: You will need an account with a reputable broker like Charles Schwab or Merrill Lynch to buy any stocks listed on either of the two main exchanges. A full service broker employs account executives in every branch or office. If you have a question of any kind about the stocks purchased through your broker, then the account executive can answer it, or will find the answer. Also, they can execute your buy or sell orders. For this the full service broker will generally charge a service fee either based on the number of shares bought or sold or the total value of your holding. A broker at a bank will usually charge a quarterly fee, whether there is activity or not.

I don't generally recommend the use of full service brokers because of the high fees they charge, (though it is my experience that the fees for services can always be negotiated lower, depending on the size of the account). I only recommend them for high value accounts where the owner cannot keep a good eye on his investments. There are certainly advantages to having an account executive to call when you want to know about a particular company or a recent news item, although nowadays I do it all online. However, a good account executive, if needed, is worth his weight in gold. He will have his fingers on the pulse of the market and can make quick decisions for your account. However, such account executives are hard to find and must be picked carefully based on their previous track record.

Personally I prefer discount brokers like Charles Schwab. I like to be involved with my portfolio account, and discount brokers allow this. You can make your own decisions as to what you want to buy and sell while at the same time you can still get some help from the discount brokers in those decisions. Many of them have very good research departments. In addition, they are fixed in their fees, which are significantly lower than full service brokers. Discount brokers charge a flat fee for each trade, often irrespective of the number of shares bought or sold. It is perhaps obvious that there would be higher costs for buying through what is called a full service broker, like UBS or Merrill Lynch, rather than a discount broker because of the differing level of service. If you are computer savvy, it is far better to go through a discount broker. They are much, much cheaper to use, and the savings can be very significant. Discount brokers do not generally charge any fee for holding your account.

When looking for a broker, don't forget that they do not like to lose customers and they will often offer special deals for would-be new customers. It costs nothing to ask and to shop around amongst several brokers.

The stock market is the best investment

In the stock market some stocks occasionally fall out of favor. Andersons used to be in the S&P until they were sued over asbestos siding. The stock has now been reduced to a low price. The well-known World Com and MCI Telephone were brought down similarly. This type of thing has happened several times in the past, almost always preceded by some spectacular claims by the company to the effect that it's doing very well! Hype means nothing! Sears and Chrysler went through troubled times in the 1960's yet so far they have survived.

Ford Motors and Delta Airways are probably the most notable companies to have had recent financial problems. A lesser known S&P 500 company called Dana Corporation found themselves in trouble as a result of Ford's retrenchments. Dana was the major supplier of car parts for Ford Motors, and when Ford went downhill, Dana lost a great deal of business. Their price plummeted to .77 cents before a fairly quick recovery to over 2 dollars per share. I purchased some at .77 as well as at the higher price the following week! Notwithstanding the occasional falling out of one or two companies, the stock market has been proven to be the very best investment for those looking long-term, or beyond a five-year investment period. Slow and steady wins the race, it is said, and this is certainly the case with stock investments. Stable, free market economies have been shown to have a long-term upward momentum, some of which is generated by the effects of inflation and some by successful management and the resulting profits. Still others benefit by the accumulation of assets or the acquisition of other companies, which in turn make the original company's stock desirable to own. This upward trend via appreciation is greater with so called emerging stocks because of their potential for growth and their development of new technology. It is less marked with already developed and larger companies, which companies tend to buy up the emerging corporations in order to remain in the forefront of their industry.

I have often been asked when is the right time to get out of stocks and move into the bond or cash market so as to have ready cash for retirement. My short answer is: never! Having your money in stocks is the best place for your money to be. This is because if you reach a point where your total assets, property, and stock market investments reach, say, one million dollars, the dividends generated equal 2% or approximately $20,000 to $22,000 per year. With this money, as well as the money you can get by borrowing against your portfolio for any emergency, you can continue to live in a manner to which you had been looking forward to for an extended period of time. The added benefit is that ten years later you will be in just as comfortable a position as previously, because your assets will have appreciated along with inflation. Assets in the stock market are protected from inflation, rising with it, so that even if the cost of living rises, so does your income!

Looking at the historical movements of the stock market, it becomes very clear that there is a steady upward bias that exceeds that of any other category of investment. It is well proven that there has been a steady appreciation in average stock prices over the past one hundred years, as the medium capitalized stocks, like those in the present day NASDAQ, become the more solid large capitalized companies. There are over 2000 well established companies listed in the main stock exchanges, each of which, as an aggregate, will steadily rise over time and beat the rate of inflation according to historical precedent.

If you do not believe this, then I challenge you to check it out for yourself. Get a back edition, at least five years back (ten years would be better) of one of the papers that lists the stocks of the Dow Jones and the NASDAQ and then pick a random number of stocks yourself. Compare the original prices of those stocks that you have selected with the present day prices. Probably there will be some name changes, because of takeovers by other companies. You may even find that the odd one might have gone out of business, or been severely downgraded in price, like Dana Corporation that was taken out of the S&P because of its price drop. Yet it will not be too hard to figure out that as an aggregate, you would have done well to have owned that random group of stocks and held them to the present.

If on the other hand you decide to liquidate your assets or in other words, sell your assets when you retire, you would be doing what many have done only to regret it bitterly later. If you were to sell your assets so as to become cash-rich, you would find that in the following ten years your cash would depreciate considerably. Your cost of living would go up, and your ability to pay would go down. The price of living is continuing to rise and will no doubt continue to do so for the foreseeable future. Therefore there is a need to keep whatever assets you may have in an inflation protected investment.

The long-term investment strategy

It is a practical impossibility to anticipate what the stock market will do on a given day. I have seen the markets, both commodities and stocks, start high or low, and end high or low, in all combinations. It is quite amazing how the market can gyrate. It is a type of gambling to try to anticipate and make a profit on what will happen in a single day, and I have yet to find day traders who consistently make enough profit to retire. If you want to take that risk every day, you should move to the floor of the stock exchange, ready to pick up and take instant advantage of any rumor or trend that comes along. Even so, it's a gamble, and besides which, being a floor trader is extremely stressful.

Anyhow, this book is not for gamblers or professionals who have their life's work solely in the various stock markets. As a private individual doing worthwhile work in other fields of endeavor, you have to get on with your own life, family and work enterprise. That is why you should follow what I call the long-term investment strategy.

People normally say that owning stocks and shares is not for the timid, but I would not agree. Historically, investing can be done in a safe and easy way. The timid investor is looking for a safe, long-term way of investing surplus money for their later life, and the long-term investing approach is the way to go about it. How is that? It is buying steadily and holding good quality stocks for the long-term—that is, for a period beyond five years.

Although this approach is as sure and safe as any you could make, it does require some level of discipline by the investor. This discipline has to do with making a commitment to save, to invest, and to let the process take its course over the long-term.

You might think that the stock market is risky, that you do not wish to lose money. But how can you lose money if you have a stock portfolio and do not sell it? Yes, of course, it is to be expected that stocks and the stock market will make movements up and down, and even that some companies will go under. However, if you think this through and look at the stock market historically, then it becomes self-evident that any portfolio that is based on having a diversified group of good quality, well-funded, and well managed stocks, picked from the S&P, will always go up over an extended period of time, despite any setbacks. The famous stock market investor Warren Buffet has been reported in the press as favoring stocks above all other investments because of their ability, on average, to generate dividends and capital appreciation between 8% and 14% (by his estimation), compounded annually. ("Compounded annually" means that each year the percentage increase is based on the previous year's value, not the original value, which means the value increases that much faster, a compounding effect.) You want the same, that is, a stock portfolio that, as a whole, rises over a period of time and which at the same time pays dividends. Later in your life and perhaps with some other income too, you will be in a good place to retire. For each $500,000 you have invested in a well balanced portfolio you can expect to receive approximately $10,000 to $12,000 dollars by way of dividends annually, and at least a further $40,000 to $50,000 appreciation in your portfolio per year averaged over time and compounded an-nually.

It is well to recognize that other investments, especially property, are subject to many unknowns, such as maintenance, taxes and capital gains taxes when you sell, whereas with stocks there is never any need to sell them because you can earn money from the dividends, and even if you need quick money, it is always possible to borrow money against the value of your portfolio. By keeping your money in the stock market and not selling your stocks your money will appreciate much more quickly than in any other way, and with very little effort.

For example, if you begin by investing $20,000 in a balanced variety of 12 to 25 stocks (which you call your "portfolio"), you can expect that in fifteen to twenty years, your portfolio will be worth in the region of $1,000,000, providing you continue to add as much as you can to your investments on a regular basis, like $4,000 to $5,000 per year, and also that there is no reduction or expenditure of the capital investment. If you reinvest your dividends along the way, you can do even better. Now $1,000,000 will equate to a total dividend payout of $20,000 to $25,000 annually with the average base value of the stocks continuing to appreciate at over 8-12% per year. This is the basis of your ever-increasing income during your retirement, with the added benefit of being able to borrow certain amounts against your stocks (though you shouldn't borrow more than 10%) for special needs, and paying it off later as it becomes convenient (by dividends or some other means). The alternative is to sell some of your stocks and face having to pay taxes on the appreciation, which I do not recommend except under extreme necessity.

Of course it is possible that an individual stock may fail for no predictable reason. However, it is unlikely that high quality stocks would do so. Over a ten year period that might be at most one out of the twenty in your stock portfolio. Even so, the others that remain in your portfolio will so outperform that the overall gain and appreciation will equal or beat any other investment that you might make.

The timid person would do well to examine some Ibbotson reports, which clearly and graphically show that the appreciation of investments in the stock market have outstripped all other types of investments over the past eighty years. They show that one dollar invested eighty years ago in the S & P's 500 high capitalized stocks, (found mostly in the Dow Jones) would have appreciated 2000 times or more. And that the same investment in medium capitalized stocks (like those found in the NASDAQ) would have appreciated over 3000 times. Warren Buffett knows this well, and has benefited from this fact in order to amass his fortune over many years.

It is interesting to note that if you had the time and facilities to "go back" sixty years and buy a pretend basket of quality stocks; picking at random from the Standard and Poor's 500 at the highest prices registered for each that year, then following the prices for this basket of stocks for each of the sixty years, you would find that those stocks would still be ahead of the average for any other comparable investment you might have made—land, houses, businesses, or other investments—and with a great deal less stress upon you. (Of course you would not realistically buy stocks at the highest price each year any more that you would or could buy them at their lowest prices.) This is the reason why I say that even the timid investor who wants to build up a nest-egg can do so with a good deal of confidence by investing in the stock market in a controlled and deliberate manner. A person can make a decision, execute it, then forget about it until they have additional money to invest, perhaps three or four months later.

Actually, looking at the markets to see how the investments are proceeding should not take place more than every three months or so, at least for the first several years. A beginning investor does not want to be worried about their investment taking a short-term downturn, nor historically should they have to.

Notwithstanding that in any ten year period possibly one of your holdings will fail, historically you can expect a big return on your investments, as said before, of something like 2 or 3% by way of dividend payments, and between 8% and 12% in appreciation, compounded annually. It is also a great plus that the only taxes you will have to pay will be on the dividends, and the profits that you realize if you sell shares of stock—providing that you do not own any mutual funds. As long as you own and control your own shares, they will appreciate as a group and this average appreciation will not be taxed until you sell, which is a great way to get some wealth without paying taxes. Of course, eventually when you die your estate will have to pay the taxes on the appreciation (depending on your tax bracket) when at your death the actual shares are sold out or transferred to another person or entity as stipulated in your will, but this is another subject for another time.

How to buy

How do you buy stocks? In order to buy stocks from the stock market you have to put an order through your broker, who is the person or entity who actually sends an order to their representative at the market to buy or sell a certain stock. No one can buy or sell any stock on any of the stock exchanges without going through a stock broker.

When buying, there is always a bid and ask price. A bid is what someone is willing to pay, and an ask price is what someone wants for each share. Until there is a time when both agree on the price, there is no purchase or sale. Whether the trade has in fact been made can be ascertained either by going onto the computer or by calling your broker. You can also ask your broker the high and low price for your stock for the day, or on the previous day, week, month or year. This information is also available on your computer, usually on an instant basis.

Nowadays all orders are put into a computer. The computer waits until there is a buyer or seller who meets your price, and when it matches, the transaction is completed immediately and your personal broker is informed that the sale/purchase has been completed (or your own computer will tell you if you have an online brokerage account with a discount broker, which is what I do). If you have an online account with a broker, you can buy and sell online using that account.

Buying stocks yourself on your computer is probably less expensive than any other way. Fortunately, the new discount brokers have a great deal of information that can be accessed online by their customers. The whole discount brokerage is set up for the customer, and it is all a no-brainer. In this case, the old saying that you get what you pay for, is not exactly true. In the case of a discount broker, you get more than you pay for. There is always a commission to be added to the cost of any transaction in order to cover the various expenses, which, in the case of a discount broker, is a fixed dollar amount. You do not want your commission to be high relative to the cost of the transaction so you need to make sure that the amount you invest each time is relatively significant, or equal to at least twenty times the commission cost. The reason for this is that the commission price is generally the same for each trade (whether buying or selling) no matter what the size of your transaction, and so the higher the dollar amount you trade, the lesser the commission price is in relation to it. For example, buying $100 worth of shares and paying a $12—or 12%—commission trade cost is on the high side. Were your trade worth $1000, then that commission of $12 would be just 1.2%. Of course, I have said nothing yet about the commissions charged by some large full service stockbrokers. They do not generally charge a fixed dollar amount, which sounds good, but they have other more expensive fees, which are considerable. Chances are that a $100 order to a full service broker would be declined, as the commission costs would exceed the purchase price. In other words, you would have to pay over $100 commission in addition to the $100 you are paying for the stock.

A commission fee of one to two percent of the purchase or sale price is acceptable for the individual investor. I myself do not recommend buying less than $500 worth of a stock at one time (due to the commission fee) except if you are successful in applying the procedure that will be described next, and which allows you to compensate for the commission cost.

You can put in for a sale price lower (or higher) than you intended, so as to pay for the commission. For example, I often trade 500 shares at a time. When setting the price, which might be acceptable to me at $2.75 per share, I remember that 500 cents equals $5, so, if my commission fee is $10 and I am buying 500 shares, then I put in to buy at two cents less than I would otherwise, or $2.73. This saves me ten dollars, which means in effect that I have not paid any commission at all. The lower price has paid for my trade cost. It is a case of working out how many cents lower is the equivalent of the commission cost and putting in your buy order at that lower price. Of course, if you miss out on your purchase because of your parsimony, then you might be less pleased. I generally have ten types of shares I am trying to get, and I get only half of them at the price I want, but that's OK. I never "chase the market" but I make my desired buy at a price that is acceptable to me. Of course it is clear that the same procedures can be used if you're selling, rather than buying, a number of stocks. Your aim in that case is to increase your sale price by the amount required.

At whatever level you want to invest, it should be a steady process of investing a given (and usually equal) amount over time. You should do this consistently by buying steadily when you can afford to, even if there is a long period between purchases. And it is generally best only to buy shares that enhance your core group of stocks in some way or which take advantage of a special situation rather than to haphazardly buy stocks here and there. In any case, only buy when you can afford to do so, and without stress. Do not buy without thought of the consequences but rather buy when the prevailing conditions are suitable and there is a good financial deal.

A diverse portfolio

Good investors do not buy one stock, but a variety of stocks, which are referred to as a "portfolio." It's important to maintain a wide variety of stocks in a portfolio. Having shares in several companies and also several types of companies, is the "investment strategy" that is key to the steady appreciation of your wealth.

When you own stock, some sectors of the market often will take the lead and the prices of some stocks will appreciate faster at certain periods than at others, but if you are diversified and have a balanced variety of stocks then your average will stay relatively the same. A severe winter may cause a shortage in gas or oil, thus raising the price of these two products and therefore the profits of the suppliers above the market average. Bank interest changes or a number of mergers can cause the market to behave differently than normal. Many factors can affect the market, but if you are diversified you will be protected.

I recommend slowly building up a portfolio that contains between 20 to 40 different stocks, preferably from the S&P, with some diversifying of areas of interest, just like the ten main sectors of the S&P 500. There is no sense in investing in two stocks that produce the same or similar product. You should ideally invest equally within each area of endeavor. In the S&P these would include consumer staples, consumer non-staples, utilities, energy, raw materials, telecommunications, financials, information, technology, healthcare, and industrials. Of course there are no perfect answers as to when and how to invest. Opinions on which stocks will rise or fall are only opinions. However, with diversification in the stock market, history has shown that you will be protected under almost any circumstance. A steady invest-ment strategy is to purchase so as to add to your position from time to time until a well-diversified portfolio of stocks is achieved, equaling, as said, at least 20 different stocks. The higher the diversification in your portfolio the better. Then you can review your portfolio from time to time and see where you want to add or change to your position.

Dollar Averaging

Many people are tempted to buy when the price is going up, on the theory that it will go higher and they will make a killing. Conversely, they are tempted to sell when the price goes down, on the theory that the price will go still lower and they will lose it all. Other people are tempted to put all their money on a "great deal," and then have none left over later for a better deal. Neither of these strategies are good; they are both risky in that they have the potential to lose you big sums. So what is the best strategy? I have found that the best approach is to use what is called "Dollar Averaging," which will give you the discipline to buy in a reasonable manner. By using Dollar Averaging, you will, over time, achieve a good position.

To begin with, plan to make all of your purchases with the same amount of money every time. This means that if you have $2,000 every six months to start investing, then you should look at getting close to a $100 investment in each of twenty stocks that you have picked for your portfolio. Rather than the purchase of a given number of shares, this dollar amount becomes the standard for all your purchases. For example, with a high priced share that is at one time $50 each, you would obtain two shares for that investment (equaling $100 total), and if the price were to fall later to $10 and you wanted to pick up some more, your purchase would be the same $100, but you would now put your order in for 10 shares. In reviewing your situation, notice that you now have twelve shares at an average price of $16.67. If you were to buy into a different company, you would still only buy $100 worth, keeping all your purchases the same price.

Of course, because of commission costs, with $2,000, you would probably concentrate on perhaps just five stocks at a time, each investment being $400 rather than the $100. This figure would depend on the amount of money you have to invest each time, but with Dollar Averaging, you should always buy each stock with the same amount of money. This will make it difficult to buy on a whim or get carried away by some momentary advice.

If you find that you are able to invest at a higher level at a later time, you will add to each of your stock holdings at a higher or lower number of shares and yet still spend an equal (although higher) amount of money each time you purchase. You continue doing this until such time that you have the amount of investment in each company (twenty of them in this case) that you are interested in. All your long-term investing should be done gradually over a period of time. I would suggest you only make a purchase at most once every three months in each of the twenty stocks you own. In this way, your average is sure to balance the highs and lows of the market. If you always invest the same approximate amount of money in each group, your average purchase price for your stocks will be consistent with the market fluctuations. You should also try to balance each of your stock picks so that you do not overload your investment in a particular stock at the expense of another.

Also remember to calculate the average of your purchases. You may wind up with just ten shares in one company that cost you $1000, and 100 shares in another company that cost you $10. This is just the way it should be. Buying in this manner with the same stock over and over will give you an overall average price when you average your purchases together. This average purchase price is beneficial because the end result will balance your total holdings.

Of course it's OK to start off your portfolio by investing in just a few companies, and adding more as you progress. Don't be in a hurry. After all, you are investing for the long-term. Your normal holding time is a minimum of five years and preferably more. Having said this, once the time is right and you have the spare money to buy, do not wait for a major pull back in the price of your stock before adding it to your investments. A retrenchment of between 3% and 6% should be enticement enough—otherwise you will always be chasing the price downswings. Dollar Averaging is the least stressful and most uniformly averaging way to add to a stock position.

What if you find later that your stock price has fallen even more *after* you buy it? Well, that's life! This type of thing is inevitable. Remember you have not lost anything because you still have the stock. According to historical precedent, it will rise again in price over time. It is important to know that finding the lowest price to purchase (or the highest price to sell) is not only very stressful, but essentially impossible. The key is that you should be consistent and reasoned in your investing.

Many people get anxious when their investment undergoes a temporary lowering in price or value, but some downturn is normal! Rather than bemoan the fact, look at it as an opportunity to dollar average your investment and to buy more if you are able. It is important to realize that no matter the state of the economy or the prices that you have paid for your investments, you only lose when you decide to sell at a price below that which you paid. Conversely you have not made any money until you sell at a price above what you paid. There are high points and low points in the market each year. Consider the low points as possible buying opportunities. The quality stocks that pay dividends will continue to pay dividends, even if the price of their stock goes lower. Please note that a lowering in price has no relation to the real value of the stock—only to its perception by others.

Often the price of the stock is influenced by the big mutual funds that have to sell or buy for whatever reason. Their actions cause a reaction in the market. The stock's price then increases or decreases regardless of the stock's inherent value. The reason the mutual funds have to sell might be because they can only hold dividend-paying stocks. This means that if a company failed to pay a dividend, the mutual fund has to sell it, even though the company might still be a good company.

This effect happened with the Ford Motor Corporation in 2005, when Ford saw their stock price plummet due to poor sales and profits in North America. Mutual funds saw the trend and sold many of their shares, thus creating a still lower share price. (A surplus of sellers over buyers usually leads to a lowering of the share price). The fact that Ford was making profits in other parts of the world did not seem to register. Ford stopped paying dividends and started making adjustments to their operations in order to become profitable again, but of course this took time.

In this case you will need to make a personal assessment as to whether a particular company is going to go out of business. In the case of Ford, the possibility seemed very remote. I decided that the drastic lowering of the stock price presented a great buying opportunity, and I did buy on a dollar averaging basis. How did this work? I had previously purchased 50 Ford shares for about $30 a share. When I saw them fall to $15, rather than panic and sell my 50 shares, I purchased 100 shares at the lower price. Then I had a total of 150 shares at an average cost of just $20. In line with the subsequent general stock downturn, Ford Motor shares continued to go down, caused by outside forces not associated with the direct management of the company. Some of the large mutual funds decided to sell first and ask questions later. This caused a further major lowering of the Ford stock, but I did not mind. I did not believe Ford was going to fold like Enron. It was and still is fundamentally a very strong company with worldwide productive assets that individually are making profits. I was therefore happy to buy another $1500 dollars' worth, or two hundred shares, this time at $7.50 per share, making my total investment in Ford to be $4,500 over several years. I now had 350 shares that I expected would eventually pay a dividend and which cost me an average of $12.88 for each share.

As of today, dividends have resumed, and the price of the stock has gone up. The moral of this story is that if you have a good quality company, even if it falls on difficult times, it is still a good investment for the long-term. After all, you are looking at ten, twenty, or even thirty years in advance for your retirement or the time when you believe you will need the money. You are in for the long haul.

Buying on margin

Buying on margin is useful for those who tolerate some level of risk; it is not for the faint of heart. Basically it is pledging some of the assets in your portfolio against some purchases that you would like to make. This would mean that, in general, for each dollar value that you have in your portfolio, your broker would allow you to buy another dollar's worth of stock up to a certain point. This is called "margining" your account. Depending on the broker, you will be able to borrow, as a maximum, anywhere between 50% to 69% of your stock on margin, leaving you with between 50% and 31% "equity" or net value. However, the maximum is not recommended. Margining your account that much can be dangerous in a severe market downturn. Once your equity gets down to 33% of the value of your account, life will become more hectic, as your broker can begin to liquidate your account unless you are able to put in extra money for a "margin call." Your broker does not want to be at risk of losing either, and there are also government rules that require certain minimum assets in a margin account.

I myself feel that a 75% equity or higher (25% or less borrowed on margin) is the best level to maintain in the normal course of events. If you have that special opportunity and you need to purchase additional shares for your portfolio, or you need to borrow some money for your own personal use (see later section), the lowest you should ever go is 55% equity, and if this is the case, you should increase your equity back to 75% as quickly as you possibly can.

I would never recommend using margin to purchase stocks when you are just beginning your investments. There is nothing worse than to borrow money on margin to purchase stocks and then see those stocks lose value, and therefore have to sell at a loss. After all, you cannot expect each of your purchased stock to move upwards as soon as you buy them. If your stocks were to lose value and you were 50% margined, this would mean that for every dollar your stock purchases went down, you would lose in effect two dollars—which would no doubt cause you some anxiety. Rather, if you want to open a margin account with your broker, it would be far better to purchase your stocks initially with cash and use your margin account to take advantage of a future downturn when it occurs. In this way you can buy a distressed but quality stock at a lower price. Besides, if you have a reserve borrowing ability in your account, it is always nice to know that, should you have a sudden emergency, you could draw on that reserve instead of having to sell any of your stock portfolio.

In a way, buying on margin is to gamble that the total value of your shares will increase in value more than the cost of the interest you will have to pay on the borrowed money. Like borrowing money from any institution (such as a bank), there will be interest charges for the money you borrow on margin, though such interest is generally tax deductible. This is not unlike the interest that you pay on a home that is mortgaged, which is close to the concept of a margin. After all, you are borrowing against an asset.

The percentage of interest on the amount margined is usually negotiable with the broker and is influenced heavily by the interest rates set by the Federal Reserve. It can be negotiated by asking what the best rate is and comparing it with others. The higher amount you borrow and the greater the worth of the stocks in your account, the lower the interest rate you can negotiate. If later you are dissatisfied with the service, you can indicate that you might go elsewhere unless they lower their rate.

The dollar amount you have on margin will ultimately depend both on your risk tolerance, and your ability to withstand a downturn in your portfolio with outside funds. You don't want to overdo it. Living up to your limit can be very stressful, and this you don't want, if your goal is to have a better, more comfortable life at some point in the future.

Buying into the right company at the right price

How do you know what to buy? And how can you buy it at the right price? Go to the Standard and Poor's 500 list of companies, where you will find that there are ten main segments represented. The benefit of picking from the S&P is that they are the pick of the pick— they are well capitalized and established companies. You want to pick at least one company, either at random or ones that you are familiar with, from each of the segments. These companies are to be part of your long-term investment vehicle.

In your selection you may feel that dividends are more important than stock appreciation, in which case pick ones that already pay dividends. (It must be said here that a company that is rapidly appreciating almost always eventually pays dividends.) If there is one of the ten segments that you particularly like, feel free to pick an extra company that is within that segment. Likewise, if there is a segment that you like less, then pick only one out of it, but you still want to have representation in all ten segments.

Assemble the stocks, preferably all from the S&P 500, that you are interested in purchasing for the long-term. The number of stocks should be *more* than the total number you anticipate buying, because next you will decide which ones fit your criteria. The criteria you should follow are:

- Avoid buying shares that are in the top price range, because there may be little room for growth.
- Do not buy any stock that is clearly at the top of a cyclical move. Wait until it has retraced lower from its highs. You can google each stock and see how it has done over the past 5 to 10 years.
- Avoid buying any stock that has a history of swings greater than 15% of its price, either up or down, during the past three years. This company may be unstable.
- Only buy companies that have been in business for many years.
- Avoid any stock that has remained essentially flat in price over the last five years. Stocks should appreciate at least 8% compounded annually over time, besides paying a regular dividend.
- You should probably favor the technology sectors of the market as they currently perform above average. Manufactured items that keep up with the latest technology and advancements are the best.
- Companies that pay a 3 ½% annual dividend are attractive even if the share price is high. It is interesting to note that when the interest rate in banks goes up, the price of many stocks tend to go down, and vice versa. People compare the rates they can obtain from a bank versus a stock, and make hurried decisions which you are not going to do. You are going to hang on to your good stocks.

- Avoid companies with a fad bias. They can do very well for a relatively short time, but eventually fade or become stagnant. These include restaurant chains, specialty clothing and grocery stores. I wouldn't buy into airlines either. Historically speaking, as a group, they are not good for the long-term investor. There are a specific few that do well, but they are hard to spot.
- Avoid companies that are exclusively advisory. While they often perform well for a time, they rarely pay dividends and often rely on hype to encourage their share price to rise. Because such companies own no tangible assets, it is often the case that the advising personnel finally sell their own shares and cash out, leaving the investors high and dry. In addition, if the advisors are good with their advice, they are financially enticed away to other companies. Eventually, such companies fade away, leaving little for the general investor.

Another thing to look at when it comes to buying into the right company at the right price is whether the chart of the company's share activity shows an uptrend or a downtrend. Look at the chart performance and the dividends of the stock that you are interested in over the previous five year period. It will give you an idea as to either its gentle but steady rise (even if the chart does have some valleys from time to time) or its general downward bias. Naturally, in deciding what stock to buy, you want the stock that shows a steady rise.

Valleys in a stock that is going steadily up indicate a buying opportunity for you, as previously stated. It's good to purchase a stock at a near bottom of a downward trend in an otherwise well-established company, more especially as a professional adviser will seldom recommend such a stock for you to purchase. Professional advisers usually only advise you to buy stocks that are in favor or in the news.

As for purchasing the stock at the right price, here is one way to go about doing so. If the chart shows a down trend extending over the previous one to three years, (which is OK if the company is basically good and pays dividends), then put in a "limit bid" which is a set price at which you will buy the stock if it reaches that point. I prefer a "Good Till Cancelled" order which is a type of "limit buy" that lasts forty-five to sixty days, depending on your broker. After that it is automatically canceled. Your set price might be the lowest price on the company's yearly chart or a little bit higher.

The advantage of a GTC (Good Till Cancelled) order is that if the stock makes a big move upwards just as you put in your order, you will automatically have another chance at its purchase later, if and when the stock makes a sudden correction downwards. You do not have to keep an eye on the stock in order to buy it at a low price. The GTC order does it for you. Of course you cannot expect to obtain every stock you are interested in, and some will get away. I usually do a GTC order when I am away traveling, especially if I want to build a bigger position in a stock which I already own.

Another, more certain way to get your stock is to put in a "day order" for just above (by perhaps half of 1%) the previous day's low. Day orders are handy when you want a stock right away and are willing to pay more for it, rather than let it get away. But you don't really want to be daily involved with the stock market, which day orders cause you to do, so my recommendation is mostly to use GTC orders.

When getting ready to buy your stocks, you should have a list of more stocks than you will actually buy because you won't be able to get all the stocks at the price you specify, and you should never chase the stocks. There is no stock worth having at any price. Remember that on average it will eventually do some retracing in its price, giving you an opportunity to buy it at a later date. My experience is that whenever I have chased a stock, going higher and higher in my offered price, it invariably went down later, even that same day. But even if it does not retrace, remember you'll be fine without it. There should be enough diversification in the rest of your stocks to keep you happily engaged with other purchases.

After you have purchased your first stock, you are able move on to another stock and do the same as with your first purchase. Keep doing this until you have your basket of stocks. Try never to put in a bid to your broker for the market price, or place an "at-the-market" order yourself if buying stock online. If you do this, you will most likely end up purchasing the stock at a higher price than you could by placing a limit order at a specified price. With a limit order, the chances are high that you will get the stock you want at a better price within the next few days.

Incidentally, most professional advisers and account executives will buy at the "market" and not bother with buying at a specified lower price. I suspect that they figure that if they are asked to buy a stock, they just buy it. This is in part due to their customers having heard some hype or popular "hot tip," so they are not happy if the requested stock isn't purchased. However, that very hype has caused the stock to rise substantially in price. I can understand the professsional side of it, but that does not mean that it is the best approach for you. Don't ever buy the stock when it is most in favor. Remember, you have a range of stocks that you are interested in purchasing.

Recently I was interested in a stock that had been recommended eighteen months earlier. The fundamentals were good, yet because of some strike action the shares had halved in value, and were being traded at $6 to $6 1/2 per share, having seen a low of $5 1/4 during the previous three months. I put in a GTC bid to buy 300 at $5 1/2. Four weeks later, during a three day moderate market downturn, I bought them for my bid price. While brokers much prefer you buy a stock at market because it's a guaranteed sale for them on the day, they will accept a different bid price and try very hard to fill it.

Although I don't recommend buying a stock at market price, even so, it will not markedly interfere with your long term plan. After ten or more years you will think you purchased it at a bargain price. The good news is that in general, what you pay for a stock has little bearing on your eventual success as long as you stay in the market for the long-term. It is going in and out, buying and selling short term, that puts people at the greatest risk of losing money and getting gray hairs. You, however, will be able to save 2% to 5% by taking your time and using the methods I have outlined. Small savings can add up, as they are compounded over the years.

If you do buy at the market, it is better to buy at the open or close of the day. This is because buying at that time represents an average price that is based on the demand at that time rather than being the highly variable price you get if you buy a stock in the middle of the day. Buying a stock in the middle of the day is more of a gamble.

Finally, do not expect to buy your stock at the bottom of the market (or to sell at the top of the market.) You cannot expect to guess the lowest point (or highest point) at any time. I can say that, out of the many thousands of trades I have made over the previous twenty years, I have managed to get the lowest price of the day perhaps three times, though I have come within two to ten cents often enough. People beat themselves up because they could have gotten it lower (or sold it higher), but the truth is that no one can predict the future. The vast majority of trades, that is, purchases or sales, are made in the middle range of the day's sales.

Selling

So what about selling? In general, especially during your initial five year investment period, you should try as much as you can to refrain from selling any of the main holdings of your purchased stocks except for dire circumstances, even if a stock goes way down (which is bound to happen occasionally). Once you have a good share portfolio, the best thing to do is to hold onto it indefinitely until the end of your life, at which point it can be transferred to a loved one. In this way this protected source of dividends will always be there to support you. You should never have to sell your stocks because if you really need money for some reason, you can borrow against them.

You will have to learn to divorce yourself from the ups and downs of individual stocks. In fact, I recommend that you do not even look at the day-to-day ups and downs of the stock market. I have quite often been reminded by a well-meaning account executive that a certain stock was doing poorly and therefore I should sell it before it went down further. The same account executive has also been kind enough to remind me that I had a good profit in another stock and should therefore sell it to take my profit. But selling a losing stock will generate fixed losses and commissions (or the fees you pay the broker to sell). And selling a winning stock generates taxable profits and commissions. Both of these take away from the money you have growing in the stock market, and will prevent your nest egg from developing as quickly. The truth is, it is better not to sell at all, or to sell only rarely.

There could be times when you see one of your stocks become an 'odd stock', due to factors you couldn't have foreseen. Even if you have put the same amount of funds into each of the companies that you invest in, you will find that, rather than each stock being equal, they have an unequal dollar percentage in your portfolio. Some will out-perform and some will under-perform and thus they will diverge from each other. It is generally considered by financial advisers that once an investment in a stock goes beyond ten percent of your portfolio value, then you should sell some of that stock and invest the proceeds into one of your lesser performing stocks, or another stock altogether. I feel that this advice is premature; after all, why penalize a stock for being good to you? To sell an out-performing stock in order to take profits can be harmful for you in several ways. Firstly you will generate taxable profits or capital gains on which you will have to pay income taxes to the federal government and also to your state. Secondly you will lose some level of forward momentum in your portfolio.

Nevertheless, if a stock out-performs toward 15% (20% at the most) of my portfolio's value, then I step in and change something, either by selling some, or by putting available funds into purchasing other stocks, which will have the effect of lowering the dollar percentage of the stock in question. Balancing the stocks in a portfolio in this way from time to time is fine, because, of course, it is prudent "not to put all one's eggs in one basket" and to have sufficient diversity in order to reduce risk.

If there's an emergency and I have to sell some stock, I usually plan to sell part of several stocks, in order to keep my portfolio balanced. Then I look at the possible capital gains, which is the difference between what I paid for the stock and what I will sell it for. The tax on capital gains varies from year to year. I will have to pay Uncle Sam between 15% and 40% of any gain. So I prefer to minimize capital gains. Not to get too complex, but this can be done by offsetting any gains with a capital loss, in other words by selling some stock for a gain, and other stock for a loss.

You can borrow money without selling your stocks

If you need some money at any time, you can pledge your shares for a loan of up to half their value. I don't recommend borrowing the entire 50% against your portfolio as this can put you at high risk if there is downturn in the market. Rather I recommend borrowing 25% at the most. For anything more than 25%, the loan should be short-term, and paid off as soon as you possibly can. Otherwise, if your margin shares go down, even temporarily, you are at risk of being sold out by the stockbroker as soon as the net value of your portfolio no longer covers the value of your loan. Lenders want to protect themselves against default.

Several good things come from borrowing money with your shares as security. Firstly, you will not have to sell your shares (and you thereby avoid paying any capital gains on any profits.) Secondly, the interest you pay on the loan is tax deductible to you. Thirdly, you can pay the loan back early or late without fear of a penalty that you cannot pay. Your shares are like gold to your lender, be it a bank or your broker. Finally, the dividends and annual appreciation of your shares are likely to exceed the amount of the interest charged.

To get a loan from your broker, you open a margin account, and just ask for some money; they will gladly give you a check the same day. You will find out how easy it is, and the added bonus is that the interest will be the lowest going rate with no borrowing fees (establishment fees, origination fees, etc). This ability to borrow against your stocks becomes even more valuable as you get older and the worth of your stocks increase, because you will be capable of using it to do special things for your family, or perhaps to go on a trip that you have always wanted to go on. The only downside to be aware of is, again, that your stocks can be sold out if you are not careful about keeping the right percentage of equity in your account, so be careful not to borrow too much and leave such borrowing only for special occasions.

How many shares to purchase

How many shares of each company should you purchase in total? The short answer is, as many as you can afford. Eventually you need to work up to a total investment that will bring in an amount that will satisfy your future yearly needs. Only *you* will know what that is. Your yearly needs will be provided by the dividends that you get from your portfolio, which should average between 2% and 3% of your investment value at any given time. This does not seem like much. However, the average appreciation of your quality stock portfolio, even if you occasionally lose one of your stocks, will be between 8% and 12% on top of your dividend. This means that if you don't sell any of your shares, your portfolio will double in value in about eight to twelve years, and, as you will see, your dividends will double also.

More on mutual funds

As I have already said, you should only buy and hold individual stocks for your long-term investment, and not mutual funds. A mutual fund is not the same as a stock, and should never be purchased for long-term appreciation. This is not to say that I disapprove of them, but for the long-term accumulation of wealth they are not the best choice.

Mutual funds cater to many diverse investor interests including environment, health, high and low capitalized stocks, indexes, technology, etc. Whatever your fancy is, for or against certain things, you are quite likely to find a fund that zeroes in on it. But just because the fund caters to some specific area of interest does not mean that it will appreciate in value. Often the opposite happens. For example, there used to be diversified funds (such as college or hospital funds) that had a wide range of stocks, including cigarette companies. Then several influential publications came out with negative reports on smoking, and suddenly there was a great outcry for boycotting tobacco companies, which were, at the time, paying good dividends and whose prices were on the high side because of their solid financial position. Many funds and financial managers were forced to sell all of their stock holdings in tobacco companies because of the outcry. People threatened to pull their investments out otherwise. The end result was that the prices for the tobacco companies' shares plummeted, but it had no effect on the profitability of the various tobacco companies, they kept on making huge profits. The shares that had to be sold at a loss by some mutual funds resulted in a significant loss to the very people who had virtuously insisted that the tobacco holdings be liquidated. The tobacco companies' shares eventually rebounded giving good appreciation to those who had purchased them at the lower prices.

It just goes to show that it almost never is a good thing to invest on the basis of your moral belief only. Though moral reasons are important, all factors should be taken into account. Investors are in the market to build up wealth for long-term benefit. Certainly if you do not like a company, you should not purchase it in the first place. However, to invest in some socially conscious or environmental company without looking at its financial viability is to neglect the essential matters. Very few socially conscious or environmental investments can make the sustained profits you are looking for on a long-term basis. This is not to say that some small investment should not be made, but not for your long-term future financial security.

As for Mutual Funds, the US laws and regulations pertaining to such funds are strict. At the end of every year, each of the registered funds has to report their financial position. They must report what they have made or lost for that year, who the owners of the shares are and a lot of other information. Also, they have to report how much each shareholder has gained or lost, which information is immediately linked to the shareholder's tax returns. The information automatically goes to the IRS and then the shareholder has to report the gain (or loss) in their own taxes which can be inconvenient if it comes at the wrong time. Perhaps you have made a habit of knowing and arranging for your taxes to be paid at the end of each year. Then suddenly you find yourself with an unexpected capital gains notification for which you have made no provision and which will influence your April taxes, both state and federal, as well as each quarterly pretax payment for the rest of the year. Would you not have preferred that the capital gains remain as a paper gain to earn more for your eventual capital base rather than being realized right now?

This is the biggest problem I have found with mutual funds—the taxing of the capital gains of the shares. Rather than allowing the gain to stay in the stocks and continue to appreciate, the gains are counted and taxed—to you. With your personal ownership of stocks, unlike a mutual fund, none of your capital appreciation (which is the amount your stocks gain in value) is taxable to you until you sell. A mutual fund has to pay tax on any paper gains it makes each year, and of course it passes this expense along to you, but with personal ownership, the gains in your unsold stock will continue to appreciate and gain value without being hampered by taxes.

Also, when you own mutual funds, you will not get paid the dividends directly as you would if you owned the stocks yourself. Rather, the dividends go into the mutual fund, and are used substantially to pay the expenses incurred by the fund. If the fund's holdings increase enough in value and they receive sufficient dividends, then the fund will make a profit, some of which will go to you, the shareholder. However, due to all the fund's expenses the profit received by the shareholders will not be as great as if the shareholders owned those same stocks in their own portfolio.

As an investor for the long haul, you can "have your cake and eat it too." If you purchase a share for $10 and it rises to $15 in five years, $22 in ten years, $50 in twenty years, you will pay no tax on the appreciation of your original $10 as long as you do not sell it. However, you will be paid an ever increasing yearly dividend throughout those same twenty years or more. The percentage dividend you get on the going share price will probably stay the same, but as the basic share price increases, so does the dollar amount paid to you, thereby generating money from the money you've already invested in order to offset and even generate gain in the ever perpetual inflation.

Because of the reasons mentioned and also the fact that many mutual funds play games in abstruse areas of the market, such as futures, hedges, derivatives, and the like, I feel that they are not the place for the serious long-term investor. Most mutual funds are geared for buying and selling short term, which I consider to be a bad thing because of the tendency towards gambling, and this is yet another reason to avoid them. The action of mutual funds wields a great deal of power in the market place just as a club wields power, but if it happens to fall, especially on your foot, it can have painful consequences!

So you want to stay 95 to 98% invested in your share portfolio of thirty to forty stocks. (I always keep a cash reserve of 3% to 5% in my portfolio account.) Do you need to worry what the market does, when you know that even the knowledgeable experts are divided as to which way the market will go from month to month? No, let others have ulcers and premature wrinkles. You need only get on with your own affairs, steadily purchasing more shares as you prudently can, as already explained, on a dollar-averaging basis. You need not worry whether the market is up or down, as long as each corporation's worth and activity are still there. Yes, there may be times when you feel strongly not to purchase additional shares of a particular stock, but there will not be many such times. Your main function, rather than being led by the crowd, or indeed even putting a lot of time into studying the market, will be like the chicken that, once having laid her basket of eggs, sits on them to see what happens, and after a while finds that her sitting has paid off.

CHAPTER SEVEN

Advanced Investing Concepts

Four-Dimensional Stock Purchasing

How do you buy into the stock market? I have observed several different strategies. In the last chapter, I talked about picking companies from the Standard and Poor's index practically "at random". Some years ago a friend handed the stock-exchange section of the newspaper to his cleaning lady and asked her to circle ten stocks at random. He followed these shares for over a year, noting the rise and fall of their prices, and found, somewhat to his surprise, that they did as well as those in his own portfolio. However, most investors do not use this random, one-dimensional approach. Ordinarily, you buy into a company because it is recommended to you through the media, a friend, or just hearing or reading about it. Then you purchase the number of shares that you can afford (or are willing to lose if things don't go as planned). I call this "two-dimensional purchasing".

Another method involves doing a little research into the quality of the company: What has been said about it? What do the financial experts think? Has it been recommended by those who have studied the company's history? What dividends are paid or have been paid recently? Have you been using any of the products manufactured by the company? How long have they been in business? I call this strategy "three dimensional."

The fourth strategy is what I call "four-dimensional purchasing". This time you go even further. You look for several other factors having to do with the fundamental value of the companies and their products.

Four-dimensional purchasing is about using a more psychological approach than is normally the case. It's about taking the long-term view.

I happened to be watching the news on one occasion and saw that Proctor and Gamble had taken a sudden plunge in share price from $76 to $57. Apparently the CEO had done or said something out of place and the market (that is, the financial experts) had determined there was something wrong with the company and that it would therefore not earn the expected profit returns for the following quarter. I figured this was only a perception and that the CEO's misstep did not indicate anything fundamentally wrong with the company. Therefore I saw it as a tremendous buying opportunity. Proctor and Gamble has been noted for its tremendous range of products that have been sold worldwide for many years. Anyone would be likely to find at least fifty of their products in any major store, items such as soap, toothpaste, face cream, etc. I thought to myself that any statement by one person, even if he were the head of the company, could not permanently damage that company. Perhaps it would become a takeover target by another company, but that's all. In this way I was thinking four dimensionally, or over time.

A portfolio manager that I knew had purchased shares at $76 and because of the negative publicity sold them at $57. He said that it was better to sell them now as the money could be put to better use in another stock and that P&G would not recover for another three years—or that is what the experts predicted. However, I purchased some P&G shares at $57 and sold them six months later at $76. To my chagrin they subsequently rose to over $100 and then split, two shares for one! Those who predicted doom for P&G were not thinking four dimensionally. You, however, can learn to do so.

Here is another example: Out of the twenty stocks that I had in my portfolio some time ago, I was heavily invested in five particular ones which I had deduced would rise significantly in price at some time in the long-term future. The purchase price of these stocks was very attractive. The stocks were Sun Micro, Corning, Motorola, Ericsson, and Williams. All my purchases had proven to be good, but these five were particularly attractive.

Sun Micro, which had been a high flyer previously, stubbornly refused to budge. It was up and then down in the $2 to $3 range. All I heard from the media was "It's not going anywhere. There are better, higher priced stocks to be bought." Despite this, I steadily added to my positions in Sun Micro. This up and down of Sun Micro went on for about two years. And here is where my four-dimensional thinking went into play. Here is a company with thousands of workers and five billion dollars in cash reserves, spending about one billion dollars each year on R&D, or Research and Development. Why are they doggedly pushing ahead with their high rate of R&D if they do not have great hopes for their future? They must sooner or later develop something positive and then the price will rise to a point of making a profit and paying dividends. Yet for months they remained in the doldrums while my Corning shares steadily gained in price so that they became 23% of my total portfolio value!

Motorola also kept staying at a low price in comparison to where it should have been. My original thinking was, "Motorola has been around for a long time. They are marketing worldwide. They have a dominant position in China where the potential for sales of Cellular phones will be tremendous in the future. The lower US dollar gives them an advantage over the competition that will be hard to counter. They have a good name. They pay dividends." I could not understand why the price of Motorola was so low. However, all shares were down in general. Perhaps, I thought, one reason they have not moved upwards is because they previously reported making a loss. But why did they make this loss? Of course! They were building new production facilities in China and Southeast Asia, which took a lot of money which they could write off as a loss. Later, I thought, it would all catch up and they could not help but make good profits. Indeed, Nokia, their rival, was doing well in China.

Then the crash of 2002-2003 happened. The market took a beating. The number of sellers was high. The volume of buyers was low. When this situation arises only one thing can happen, which it did. The prices went down. The more the stock market goes down, the more momentum there is for dropping further until there is a virtual flood of sellers. Money for buying dries up because it is not possible to buy on margin any more.

In the case of Motorola, margin calls for stocks that sank below five dollars added to the pressure to sell. Stocks that went below three dollars cleaned up any remaining margin because stocks below certain prices cannot be used to borrow money for purchases of other stocks (i.e. margined), so many shares had to be sold to meet the margin demands by the brokers.

It was painful for those squeezed in the middle. Mind you, this drop in the market had little to do with fundamentals. The good stocks were still good, but the good stocks suffered along with the bad ones. It was a circumstantial occurrence, not a fundamental flaw in the companies themselves.

At the time, I went through a learning curve. My thinking was, "I have to sell some of my stocks in order to survive, and I need to get out of the major portion of my margin account in order to reduce my dependence on it." A portfolio manager advised me to sell the lower-priced stocks. However, I felt that it would be better to do the reverse, to sell all or most of my high- priced stock in order to protect the quantity of shares that I had (or could get) at the lowest prices, even if they were not marginable. After all, my lower-priced stocks were all very sound companies that had been around for many years, Corning and Ericsson being the best of them.

So during the worst of the 2002–2003 market crash, I did sell some assets and borrowed money to cover margin costs. Fortunately, I had maintained a very good credit rating and was able to accumulate enough money to maintain some level of buying of the very low, beaten down shares like Williams and Ericsson, both of which bottomed out at 27 and 37 cents respectively. Here again my four-dimensional thinking told me that there was no way that either of them was going to disappear. There was bad news, panic, and selling all around, but I learned that it was a good time to buy.

I am now convinced that holding onto good stocks and/or buying them at the low is the best way to invest. Williams had many assets in oil pipes; Corning had great infrastructure in buildings, equipment and staff; Ericsson was 46% owned by the Swedish government. Even though the future will always be uncertain it is better to be ruled by facts than by panic! It is also good to have very few, if any, purchases made on margin. This is a big part of four-dimensional thinking. Also, it is trusting in the facts and your personal knowledge, not the temporary side issues. It is trusting that a certain company is a good one and will not go out of business, even when investors are panicking. Good investors need to be able to think independently and outside the box. Mutual funds may have to sell for their own reasons, but the ordinary investor does not! Which is another reason why managing your own stocks is the best thing to do.

So what happened to the companies I invested in? Williams's management had made some bad decisions, over-extended themselves, and had to sell some of their assets in order to get into a better financial situation. Within this time period, the market's selling pressure was intense. Fortunately they had managed to keep most of their core assets. I could see that they were going to survive and I managed to pick up a quantity of stocks near the low point of the downward movement. I picked them up at 27 cents. They later condensed the shares by doing a ten to one reverse split, thus each ten shares became one share at $2.70; within one year these shares had significantly increased in price and continued to go higher afterwards.

Corning was a different case. The lawsuits that were outstanding against the company were huge, all because of the failure of one of their fiber-optic products. *Sell, sell*, said all the conservative mutual funds and others. However, when looking at their assets, their profits, and their forward planning as well as the fact that they were a 150-year-old company, it was clear to me that the low price had no relation to the value. Here again I purchased and kept on purchasing the stock as it went up. At the time of writing it is a well-respected company, making very good profits and on its way to doing even better. My original purchases at around $5 a share have more than quadrupled.

Ericsson had been a well-respected Swedish technology company, but had made the mistake of gearing up for a certain quantity of electronic equipment which it found that it could not sell. It was going to mean a huge loss to them. Naturally the experts wanted to have nothing to do with it and within a period of three weeks there was a positive flood of selling which snowballed the stock from the high teens all the way down to 37 cents. Yes, that is the price at which I purchased them. Soon after they condensed each of their shares by a factor of ten, just as Williams had done, which meant that my 25,000 shares at 37 cents converted to 2,500 shares at $3.70. Within three weeks the shares had more than doubled in price. I did not sell because I knew that once they had cleared their obsolete inventory, they would be back on track for success. Indeed they later reached over $40 at one stage. The dividends that they pay are almost equal to my original price of 37 cents, so why should I sell and pay a large capital gains tax and lose dividends?

As for Sun Micro, it was a disappointment for me. Still, one out of four is not too bad. I am still waiting for the price to make a big upward move. It eventually changed its tactics and used its money and expertise to get into a better place. The price moved a little higher, and who knows what is in store for the future? I have not lost money in Sun Micro. I did finally sell it at a modest profit. Thinking outside the box does not mean you will be right 100% of the time.

As you can see, four-dimensional thinking enables one to isolate the panic in connection with a stock and look at the real situation. It requires you to do some reading about the company's past, present and future, which is easily done online. You can consult publications like the Wall St. Journal, Business Week, or the US News and World Report. Ibetsons and Barrons are also respected business publications. You can look up the latest company's report on their website. It means that you hesitate and think before you buy. It also helps if you know something about business in general and the necessary balance between assets and liabilities such as inventory purchases, labor costs, and the like.

I have found it better to add to my already-held positions which I can observe over time, rather than have a scattergun approach and buy into more and more companies. Having 30 to 40 different stocks seems to be a maximum amount to look after. Many times I have seen a sudden collapse in a stock's price (such as Sherwin Williams, Caterpillar, Proctor and Gamble, and many others) where I have known that the company is basically good. However, I keep away from small companies with no proven track record. Sure, there is always the possibility of making a wrong decision, like with Enron or World Com. There is no way of avoiding the occasional "bad egg" of top management, when the company has falsely reported their true position. Yet fortunately these crooks are few and far between and do not affect the overall advantages of investing in the stock market.

More on thinking four dimensionally

There are several things to look for when investing in a company's stock and when trying to determine if it is a good, solid company; be aware of the following:

The debt of a company

What is the debt of the company? Almost all companies have some level of debt. Debt is not necessarily bad. If an overall good company borrows money for expansion and pays 10% interest annually for their capital but makes 20% profit, then this is a good strategy, especially considering that any interest they pay to the lender is fully tax deductible to them. You can find out this type of information on the internet, in the company's annual report, or by phoning the company's investor relations for more information (every listed company has one).

The length of time in business

How long has the company been in business? It is a very definite plus if the company has been in business for ten or more years. This would mean that it has some stability, more especially if the chart shows a generally upward trend.

The look of the chart

How have the shares performed over the past one to three years? Look at the five-year chart when you first investigate. What do you feel about them? They tell a story; each story is different because each company is different, with various products and services. Is there an upward movement in share price? Dividend payout? General sales? You are not looking for a huge rise, but if you see a general upward trend, slow but steady, that's good.

It is fine to look at as many companies as you can. You do not have to invest in them all, only the best of them. If you don't do this research, you may miss out either on an opportunity to buy or, conversely, a necessity to sell. If you see two or more downward spikes in the price, find out why this is so. Just one spike per year is generally no cause for alarm. Most stocks have occasional spikes downward that are usually technical rather than fundamental. A downward cliff could indicate a split (like a two for one) which is normally a good thing because the stock becomes more tradable; the downward cliff could also be an indication of a large stockholder or some mutual funds that needed to sell. However, if there are two downward spikes near to each other you should find out the reason; in this case the spikes down could well be fundamental. Your stockbroker can tell you.

Instead of a spike down, you may see a spike up. This could happen because of people who have "shorted" a stock, betting that it would go down but then they have to buy it back to cut their losses because the stock goes against them. Or it could mean that the company has done a reverse split (like one for two), causing their share price to suddenly be higher. There are many reasons why there could be a spike up, and it all has to do with supply and demand. The main reason to be aware of the spikes up is so that you do not go and buy a share at the peak only to find that it suddenly spikes down again later. You always want to buy at the low.

I remember the time when I looked at the chart of RAMBUS. It showed a regular rhythm of spikes up followed by retrenchments to the original price. It seemed to me that it occurred at fairly regular intervals. By projecting these intervals forward, I was able to purchase quite a number of shares near the lowest price, then sell them for about double what I had paid for them. My involvement with RAMBUS had nothing to do with any long-term wish to purchase, as they did not pay any dividend at the time. I was just taking advantage of a situation that I saw. I did this on two occasions and made some good profits that offset some of my margin interest expense. For the long term, however, it is best to avoid stocks with violent swings up and down during its history because such a pattern shows some market instability.

What if you see that the line of the chart goes steadily up, but the company does not pay dividends? Dividends are important, but this type of company would be fine to invest in and the pattern is a good sign. The company is probably using its profits for expansion rather than for dividends. The market recognizes such companies and looks at their increasing worth, which in turn is registered in the stock's appreciation. These companies can be ideal to buy because the stock is likely to appreciate nicely over time.

What if the trend of the company is flat? If they do not pay dividends then this is a negative sign because it indicates they are a non-performer. Some companies pay their top management large salaries and bonuses rather than paying dividends. Even if they do pay some dividends, they are still not recommended because they are in a holding pattern and could go up or down, and you can't tell from past performance which way they will go.

Remember that for long-term investing you want companies with market stability (as revealed by charts with few violent price swings), increasing profitability (as shown by a line that goes steadily up) and, preferred but not required, the regular payment of dividends.

Price

What are the underlying reasons for the stock's present price, either high or low? Mismanagement may cause a stock to go down at least temporarily. A takeover by another company may cause the stock to go up, even permanently. Here I must again caution any investor not to buy any stocks at their high, as the potential for the price to go lower is then very great. When one is at the top of a mountain, all one can do is to go down, unless of course there are higher mountains to climb. So it is with a stock's price.

Area of business

What is the stock's area of business and is it in demand? If it's in the area of technology and the technology is well known to you and is progressing, that is a plus. But if the company products are not in demand, then avoid it because you can't second guess what the company may or may not do or what the public will or will not buy.

Intuition

How do you feel about the particular stock that you are considering buying? If you naturally like a company, or what they produce, or you have a relative who works there and you both feel good about it, then go ahead. If you have any doubts, you should perhaps wait. The truth is, there are so many stocks out there you shouldn't have to buy one you aren't sure about. There will be many you *are* sure about. Don't agonize over a stock. If you have a good feeling about it, buy it. If not, put it aside for a later look.

More on investing wisely in the stock market

Buying stock from the company itself

These days, buying a company's stock is relatively easy. Sometimes it is possible to buy directly from the company itself. They will sell you the necessary number of shares that you want at the closing price on the designated market day (which is of course unlikely to be the lowest price of that day.) Only a limited number of companies do this, so it is unlikely to become your habit. However, this can be a good way to start a portfolio if you have only a few dollars to invest because you save the commission that is normally charged for buying shares. Nevertheless, to buy a stock just because it costs you no fees is surely a poor reason to invest. Besides, the range in prices for a listed stock in a given day varies so much that in saving a penny you might lose a dollar. Also, there may be a minimum or maximum number of shares that you can purchase—each company will have different restrictions. Finally, you may not have the option of selling the stocks back to the company. You could of course sell them on the open market, providing there is no restriction placed upon them by its company. I personally feel that to buy stocks from companies directly is likely to restrict your options for long-term investing. I have seen such services offered, but I've never participated.

High flyers

Is the stock a high flyer? Sometimes there are stocks with lots of reported upside potential. If so, who is saying it? Be very careful of these, because for every buyer (that is *you)* there is also a seller who has private reasons for persuading you to buy. Furthermore, any present high flyer is likely to have already attracted a following of buyers, a momentum which cannot be maintained indefinitely. So, even if you like the stock, wait until it retraces from its present price by at least 10%. Preferably buy another well-funded stock that is not in the limelight.

Do not get caught up with the crowd in buying or selling. If you see lots of new information on a particular stock, do not buy it, it is too late. It is too much in the limelight for purchase at this time. If you look at the recent yearly or three-yearly chart of its performance and you see that there is a recent spike upwards, then do not chase it. These up-spikes in the price of a stock have a great tendency to make down-spikes within a few months.

TV recommendations

I must caution you to avoid being dragged into listening and taking action on what TV and other financial news media say. They are primarily interested in short-term profits, either from selling shares that they do not have (shorting the market) or buying during a short-term dip in a stock. It can be very stressful if you try to follow what they do or what they suggest. It's a form of gambling which I do not recommend, especially if you intend to amass a healthy nest egg for your future.

The media are employed to inform and entertain. Their interest in long-term investing is generally limited. Long-term investing does not have the day-to-day excitement that daily trading provides, and so these programs only occasionally provide information suitable for long-term investors. How can they do otherwise? They recommend a stock only when it has already shown upward movement, too often at the highs. It might be a good stock, but as I have said, you should wait until later for its purchase. There will likely be a number of occasions when the same stock can be purchased at a lower price, usually when there is no one proposing its purchase.

On another note, you will hear mention of hedge funds, derivatives markets, and all manner of mutual funds and other financial instruments too numerous to mention. They can be a trap for the ordinary investor. These types of complicated money-making schemes come and go, and they also require a lot of time and effort to understand, let alone manage. It is better to avoid them altogether (see my previous comments on mutual funds in the previous chapter). Go into that area of the market with great hesitation if you must and not too deeply at that!

A company's area of business

What a company does can be as important as what they do not do. If you hate gambling or smoking, then it would seem that you would avoid any company that is involved with them, even if they are well established and pay high dividends. Yet it's not as easy as that. Many companies are extremely diversified and have a wide range of products that they market. If a company has many products, yet sells one item that you do not like, is it grounds for not investing in it? No, it's not!

The other side of the coin is you might love alternative energy and companies that are involved with solar or wind power. In this case, while your views might be laudable, make sure your company does not have a history of failure. Often they do not pay dividends, and their stock value erodes over the years. If you did invest, you would be taking a high risk, which is not a good plan for your retirement. Hoping for something is no basis for investing, you need some positive facts. Historically, alternative energy companies do not do well. Do you want to make a political statement by losing nine-tenths of your investment? Thinking that something is a good thing (or a bad thing) does not make it a good (or bad) investment.

International companies

Some international companies are fine in a portfolio; however, there are two types: those that are based in the United States and those that are based elsewhere. For long-term investing, you want a stable monetary system which means you do not want your portfolio's value to be overly influenced by international exchange rates which constantly change. Chance may prove that your company is good, yet because of poor exchange rates between your country and the other, the stock loses value rather than gains it.

A clear example of this is with Brazil. Had you been exposed to a good company in Brazil, your investment would have been severely reduced almost overnight when Brazil's monetary collapse occurred in the '80s and then again in the '90s, more especially if your investment had been bank related as the value of bank stocks fell dramatically due to the severe depreciation of the Brazilian currency. Who knows or can predict a crisis like this in another country? No one can, although there are tell-tale signs that can point to this possibility, such as an excess of strikes, civil unrest, or high inflation to name just a few.

At least if your money is centered in your home country there is relative stability in the value of the currency. I have noticed over the years that most of the gurus of finance who predict the necessity to invest abroad have been ultimately wrong. However, companies that are based in your home country and yet have some of their sales and income derived from overseas are OK, as you will have the best of both worlds with little or no exposure to a downturn in foreign markets.

How to manage a downturn

Because downturns are unpredictable but inevitable, I only recommend borrowing or buying on margin up to 25% of the value of your portfolio, except on rare and special occasions. Since a downturn is inevitable in a five-year-or-more investment time frame, you will then be at risk for a "margin call." This means you will be required either to put more cash into your account or to sell some of your stock. A margin call occurs when the total value of your portfolio shrinks to one-third or less of its previous value. Stockbrokers are forced by regulations to sell some of your portfolio to maintain its 33% market value if you have purchased anything on margin. If you have only borrowed 25% you are usually safe. Remember, quality stocks have a bias for an upward trend over the long term, but it is two steps forward and one step back.

It is easy for investors to get driven by the market: happy when it goes up, worried when it goes down. But this need not be. You can teach yourself to buck the trend and buy happily when it goes down. Not an easy thing to do when "Chicken Little" says the sky is falling. Here's how it works: Severe downturns are often spaced several years apart and occur as a result of a major world event such as an assassination or an attempt to disrupt the country, even fraud! Mutual funds are likely to get the bad (or good) news first, as they have their hands on the pulse of the market. They would be the first to sell. The ordinary man on the street would be the last to hear. To sell at this stage is the very worst thing to do, whereas to buy is the very best.

Any market (or even stock) that had a drop of 5% to 15% in one day gives you a wonderful opportunity to pick up some good stocks at bargain prices.

The types of occurrences that cause downturns are many and varied so that they cannot be foreseen. When they happen, suddenly there is a dearth of buyers and a surplus of sellers, both of which feed upon themselves, taking out those who have put "limit losses" on their stocks. Never put a limit loss on your selling a stock. It sounds good because it defines the price that you do not want your stock to go below, meaning it will be sold if it ever reaches that price. With a "limit loss", your stock can be sold very quickly, often for under your stated limit. The sad thing is that you are likely to find that within the next week or so, your sold stock has recovered to near its original price. I have seen this happen on many occasions. You should decide when to sell, don't let the market dictate. As I have said, it is always best to ride the market out. Have faith in the stock market. If you are in it with your own picked stocks for the long term, why worry? You have not lost any money in the stock market until you sell at a loss!

The truth is the market is naturally somewhat volatile. This is caused by many things. For example, there is the constant selling of people's estates which makes for some arbitrary price fluctuation. I suspect that the shares of a deceased estate are all sold together on the same day, often in the morning and at the market. "At the market" means that the order is to sell without regard to any higher or lower price that may be obtained. The order goes in to sell, which means *now*. The gyrations of the market in a given day can indicate this has happened. I have seen a tendency for lower prices in the morning, often, I suspect, because of orders to sell "at the open", which means getting a price that reflects the average of the opening prices. Some mutual funds always buy or sell at the opening or closing prices for the day. They like to standardize their procedures.

Another factor that creates volatility in the market is the buying or selling of what is called "a block of shares" owned by an individual holder or a mutual fund that has decided to sell all, or a large portion, of their holding in a particular stock.

It is well to understand that in the market there is also a lot of involuntary selling. I have noticed this type of selling in the morning. I suspect there are several reasons for this. First, involuntary selling is caused by mutual funds that need to liquidate shares in order to generate cash for investors. Second, if there is a severe drop in the market, or even in an individual company, those who have purchased shares on margin and who are up to their limit of borrowing power may find that they are forced by their stockbroker to sell unless they can inject cash into their account in order to meet the margin call. Look for this to happen on the third to fifth day after the beginning of a severe downward move in the market. This is your special buying opportunity.

I have noticed that the daily movements in stock market prices tend to have a pattern, starting off at a given average price, then going lower or higher by midday, then coming back closer to the opening prices by the end of the day. This phenomenon is driven by daily traders and mutual funds who are trying to capture an intraday swing to their advantage. They are trying to predict the up and down swings, but it is only a gamble—one I do not recommend. You should not be worrying about whether the stock market is going up and down each day because historically it has been shown to go up in the long term, and that's all that need concern you.

Should you sell at any time then? The short answer is no. Of course if you have lots of appreciation in some of the stocks you own and want to build up some cash reserves for when there is a particular opportunity in a downturn, then sell a few of your shares at a high point to enable yourself to have extra cash for that special opportunity later. However I do not recommend this as a typical procedure.

Here I must add a caution. If a sudden severe price drop happens to just one of your stocks, you do need to research the reasons why that particular stock has "tanked". How long has it been in business? What assets do they have? How many employees worldwide? What is the nature of their business? Answering questions like this will tell you if there is some long-term substance in the company and will reveal if the price downturn is just a short-term technicality. Even if it is a long-term problem, you may still want to hold on to it because you've only lost the money on paper. Remember, you don't lose anything until you actually sell—the stock could still go up. Keeping it to sell later will also give you an opportunity of taking a loss (if it remains low) when you need it to offset a taxable profit from elsewhere. This would normally be done in December just before taxes are sent in, and is a legitimate way of limiting your tax liability.

Finally, although nobody likes to lose a stock completely, history tells us that within a ten- to twenty-year period, any group of twenty to thirty stocks is likely to have at least one stock tank and even be delisted, that is, taken off the particular stock exchange list. The fact that it was a good stock, even listed in the Standard and Poor's prestigious 500, is not a guarantee that it will never fail. I have seen it happen several times and the reasons are legion, from fraud to natural disasters. But this is nothing to concern you unduly. In the long term, the majority of stocks in your portfolio will, based on historical precedent, outperform inflation and give you an average appreciation that will please you very much.

Prevailing world conditions and starting a portfolio

What are the prevailing world conditions at the present time? While the world is always somewhat in turmoil, there are degrees. Generally the nearer to home the turmoil is the less you would be advised to invest in stocks until things have settled down a little, unless the stock market has already dropped in which case have a go and begin to buy.

It is easy to be enthused and invest all your money in one day, but this would be a mistake. Take your time and build up your investment over a period of time, not all at once. You will be more likely to get an average that will please you. To carry out your first investments over a period of one to twelve months is less stressful than to do it in one week. How sure are you that you have entered the market at precisely the time when all your purchases will go up? It is just not possible to pick the best time to invest in any particular stock. Slow and steady wins the race.

Recommended stocks

When investing, be wary of recommended stocks. Those promoted over the internet or by fax from paid salesmen are to be avoided at all costs unless you like to be scammed. Read the small print. Do not invest in them no matter what is said about the particular stock. If it's any good, why would they need to approach you? The real professsionals would have got hold of it. No, once you get this type of solicitation, it is too late to buy. You say that the stocks are a great deal at just 29 cents, and if you buy just 3000 of them they only have to go up another few cents and you could make a lot of money! The scammers also can make a lot of money when they sell their lot to gullible people and thus bring the price down by 3 cents. This is no way for you to start serious long-term savings.

Penny stocks

Penny stocks sound as if they should have lots of potential. The thinking is to buy a lot of lesser quality shares at a very low price, and they only have to go up a little to have your investment multiply greatly! However, while I have participated, neither I nor anyone that

I have known has ever made money on such stocks—rather the reverse (especially in mining stocks). The problem with penny stocks is that often the major shareholders are interested in ways that they can get the share price higher so that they can then sell a big block of them and make a lot of money. They then buy all of their shares back again when the shares go down and try to repeat the cycle. To achieve this rise and fall, questionable methods are often used, bordering on the criminal.

When I was living in Australia a certain firm contacted me about a new type of wind-powered generator I had invented. This company said that they were interested in developing it and would like to discuss this with me. A representative visited me in Devonport, Tasmania, where I happened to be living at the time, and inspected my working prototype. He proceeded to offer me a very fine contract that essentially said a lot and promised nothing. The contract said that I would give them the rights to manufacture and promote my invention. However there was no down payment, nor was there any provision for yearly minimum payments. I suspected a mini scam, so I looked into their share volatility and price swings. They had had over the years several projects, all of which had been highly publicized in the media. This all coincided with the upsurge in their share's price. I could see that their share price was in one of its troughs, just ripe for a new promotion—my wind-powered generator! Later I visited a representative of the company in Sydney. When I suggested that the company should shoulder some of the patent expenses and costs, the proposal was turned down. The representative said that I would make so much money that I would not know what to do with it, if I would only do what they wanted. This was a red flag to me. It again indicated that there was a scam afoot. I came to believe they were trying to do what they had done in the past: make their shares go up so they could then sell the stock at the high, at which point, if I were involved, they would dump my invention and leave me with nothing. Such is too often the way with penny stocks. Be very careful with touted future riches from buying these questionable shares.

Don't buy high and sell low

Don't forget: never buy high and never sell low! When a company's shares are low, think through the reasons for their being out of favor, especially any reason why they should go out of business. The companies that immediately come to mind are many and varied: Sears, Chrysler, Ford, Delta Airlines, Dana Corporation, Sherwin Williams, Corning, Williams Corporation, and Ericsson. All have suffered severe drops in share prices at some time or another, sometimes for years on end. Yet with the right approach, most of them became great long-term investments! This is what you want to remember when a stock you own goes to a low price.

When a company's shares are at the bottom or in a valley, history tells us that the probability of them going up is greater than their going down further. Conversely, when a company's shares are high the probability of them going down is greater than their going higher. Therefore, never feel that you just have to buy a stock when the price

is high. If you buy a hot company when its shares are at the top of a mountain peak, you are likely to see the shares drop soon after, even if they go up a little more before doing so.

What not to invest in

Do not invest in companies that are in the categories of restaurants or specialty stores: air transportation, consulting companies and the like. Restaurant and specialty companies are generally too changeable and do not often stay around for the long term, though they may be good companies while they operate. The share price of air transportation companies tends to fluctuate widely because of costs of fuel and passenger load. I invested one time in Delta, but much of my investment was eventually wiped out by the re-organized company issuing new shares and giving them to management and staff while canceling all previously issued shares and making them non-tradable. Not a very nice thing for Delta to do to their investors, especially those who had been with them long term.

The only real risk

When picking stocks to purchase, the only real risk is that the company might go out of business and the shares become worthless. This is why it is necessary to correctly assess the possibility of each company going belly up. The signs that a company may go under are important to know. For instance, a low-priced stock in the S&P 500 might be a sign of the company's internal trouble. Here are some additional signs to look out for. You can research them in the company's reports or, even easier, ask your broker. Asking the right questions will be very helpful to both of you.

1. If reported debts exceed assets, this would be a negative sign for a short-term investment, but for a long-term approach it is not necessarily so. I have noticed that short-term debts in certain companies may be correctly stated, yet the assets may be understated. For example, a large company may have purchased a great deal of land and property that are on the books at cost, but some ten to twenty years later these assets will have risen considerably in value. K-Mart, when it took out bankruptcy some years ago, comes to mind in this regard.

2. A steady but persistent downtrend in the share price over an extended period of time shows that something is fundamentally wrong. It may be corrected in the long term, but still this type of company should generally be avoided.

3. Scandals are upsetting to the market. Betting against the odds is a bad idea and very risky, as the chances of such a company going through radical changes is high. Such occurrences often take time to work themselves out, if the company doesn't go under first. Avoid companies with scandals until the company has fully recovered (if they ever do).

4. While non-payment of dividends is not significant in a growing company, any company that has been paying dividends and then suddenly ceases to do so indicates that something is not right or has changed. You need to know the reasons for this before investing.

5. I have found that any company that is controlled by an individual or family group is subject to some level of volatility and potential scams. Any long-term investment may be at risk due to the needs of the individual or family group. In other words, the needs of the family will come before the needs of outside shareholders. I have never been successful investing in closely held companies that are listed on the stock exchange. ('Closely held' means that a few stockholders own most of the company.) They are often run more like a private company.

6. A consistently low share price is not good to the short-term or long-term investor because it indicates that the company is struggling and is more at risk for going out of business.

7. Any company that has a low capitalization (defined as their share price times the number of shares outstanding) or low total assets can be suspect. Of course, every company generally starts out with a relatively low capitalization and, depending on the company and its position in its field, could be a great possibility for long-term growth and therefore for long-term investment. However, there should be a clear upward trend each year. Wal-Mart and Home Depot come to mind as being in this latter category in that they started out with a low capitalization but grew to be substantial and very successful.

8. Those companies that start up with some specialty marketing scheme, like innovative foods or drinks, can be good stocks for a period of time—generally within the first two years—after which they often lose steam and their share prices tend to be flat or descending. Certain restaurant and coffee house chains come to mind. The expansions often get top heavy and some retrenchment becomes necessary. They run their course and then fade. There are exceptions, such as McDonalds, but it is only one out of at least a hundred. Therefore, for the long term, investing in such companies is not recommended.

The key to the forgoing is to consider all of the positive and negative aspects of each company before making a decision whether to invest in them.

The beaten-down company

What is a "beaten-down company"? It's a company that has been operating well for years and then for a number of reasons takes a nosedive. This drop in share price is not caused by something fundamentally wrong with the company but rather by a perception in the market.

Some past examples of beaten down companies are:
- Sears, a well-known retail store of general merchandise.
- Chrysler, a well-known automotive manufacturer.
- Erickson Wireless, a Danish manufacturer of electronic equipment.
- Williams Company, a producer and distributor of natural gas.
- Corning, a manufacturer of fiber optics and electronics.
- Motorola, a well-known maker of electronic equipment including cell phones.
- Delta Airlines, a well-established airline company.
- Ford Motor Company, a well-known car manufacturer.
- Dana Corporation, a supplier of parts for the automotive industry.

There have been many beaten-down companies over the years, some of which have gone out of business, usually not because of something wrong with the company itself and its products but rather because of greed, corruption, or some kind of gross mismanagement. Enron and WorldCom are two examples, both of which resulted in court cases. There are various other circumstances that make a particular company less attractive to investors and mutual funds, and consequently which persuade them to sell. If the price drops to a certain level it initiates a snowball effect. The mutual funds bring the price down quickly due to their internal regulations to sell. Also, the media jumps on the bandwagon by widely publicizing such events and causing even more people to sell, which further contributes to the downward price of the stocks.

So what are some of the possible circumstances that come against such companies?

- There is a slowing demand for their product or services, either through mismanagement or perhaps because management has overextended itself.
- Management has been so entrenched for such a long time that they have lost the original dynamic attitude that got their business started in the first place.
- The company has created added infrastructure to supply a market that is suddenly not there.
- The company has surplus parts and supplies that they cannot sell, either now or later. They are out of fashion or superseded by better models.
- The company has lowered or suspended the payment of its normal dividends.
- There is some sort of major conflict within upper management divisions or even with outside shareholders.
- Management has allowed their unions to dictate pay and benefits for the employees to the point that the company cannot maintain its activities in the foreseeable future.
- The company has been undercut by another company and sees that their operations cannot carry on at the current expense levels. In other words, their profit has evaporated and income does not meet expenses.

Investors speculate on the reasons why a company is not doing well or will not do well. Often the market ends up reflecting their fears. The fact that the company's problems might be temporary is neither here nor there to them. Mutual funds especially do not often wait for a future recovery because of their fears. They would rather get out now and only come back when the issue is resolved.

Although I don't recommend selling a stock in a downturn, I must advise that if you're worried about a stock, sell it. Don't lose sleep at night wondering if it will go lower. You're an investor, not a gambler. Get rid of it. However, in my experience, very few stocks become worthless. A well-established company has assets: real estate, build-ings, machinery, etc. If they become very beaten-down, they may sell out to another company, but the new company will issue you new shares to replace your old ones.

One last word on Mutual Funds

On the stock exchanges, there is a ratio of about 4 mutual funds to one actual US company (not counting penny stocks, only counting the substantial, well-run companies). That is, there are roughly a little more than 2000 listed companies on New York stock exchange and more than 8000 mutual funds similarly listed. The mutual funds have to feed off the 2000 stocks. Just this fact should give us pause as to investing in mutual funds. But the point is, this massive amount of mutual funds can have great sway over the prices of stocks. They have tremendous buying influence because of the number of them

that exist and the large quantity of stock that they hold. This influence is what can often create what I call a "technical crash" of a company's stocks.

How do mutual funds cause a technical crash? It really comes down to the internal rules and regulations that govern them. For example, a S&P 500 mutual fund can only buy or sell the 500 stocks in the S&P, they cannot own any stock that is not in the S&P. This means that when a stock is taken out of the S&P (and every year there is some adjustment to it—it is not static) the mutual fund *has to sell* the stock that is being vacated and *must buy* the stock being put into the S&P! There is, therefore, a constant juggling match going on. Whatever stock has been kicked out of the S&P has been removed because it has failed to keep ahead of the others for whatever reasons. After it is kicked out, because of mutual funds selling it, the price of the stock goes even lower. On the other hand, the stock being put into the S&P goes to a higher price just because of mutual funds buying it.

Mutual funds also create limitations for themselves in other ways that affect their stocks' prices. For example, some mutual funds have a rule not to have stocks valued below five dollars; others have lower limits, such as $4, $3, $2, and $1. It has been my observation that there are extremely few mutual funds that are allowed to hold quality stocks whose value has dropped below $1.00. For instance, Rite Aid's stock fell to 27¢ although it is now over $6. Mutual funds are unlikely to put Rite Aid into their portfolios unless it climbs even higher. They don't like to own stocks, even established ones, that have ever gone so low.

By thinking things through logically you can deduce that some stocks, when out of favor, are being clobbered by mutual funds that are forced to sell due to the internal regulations. For example, take Ericsson Wireless, a worldwide company whose shares have in the past traded at over $20 and which is 40% owned by the Swedish government. At one time they made some miscalculations and produced too many electronic instruments which they then could not sell. It became obvious that the whole inventory was going to be a write-off and they were about to lose a lot of money which would prevent them paying any dividends. When the news came out, the first reactions came from mutual funds which concentrated on dividends and had to sell. The next were savvy mutual funds that could smell a downward trend and sold out in anticipation. Next came individuals who saw their stock halved and decided to get out. Afterwards, there were those who had margin calls and were forced to sell. Once the stocks came crashing down, mutual funds that were not permitted to hold stocks at prices lower than $5 had to bail out and took their losses as well.

Here again, I must interject that the only reason for the sell-off to low levels was because of short-term circumstances. It had nothing to do with the fundamental value of the company. The Swedish government remained the biggest shareholder. There were still thousands of employees, many of them highly skilled. There was still the infrastructure, such as buildings and property, as well as raw materials and highly sophisticated machinery. Sure they had lost a lot of money, but it was not the end of the world for them by any means.

However, in a short time the Ericsson shares became an avalanche of selling. When they went below $1, I put an order in for 25,000 shares at 37¢ and got them. The price has since risen by a factor of ten.

Therein lies one of the problems with mutual funds. Because of certain rules and regulations, and perhaps a fear of being sued, they are forced to liquidate instead of examining the situation from outside the box. Individuals within these institutions are usually fearful of making wrong decisions which would jeopardize their jobs. Quite a normal human reaction that we may all have at one time or another!

Now let us look at this situation from your point of view. Suppose you purchased $500 worth of shares in Ericsson at $20 each and thus received 25 shares. You purchased the shares because you liked the company and knew the important facts, as outlined above. You were aghast at the sudden and precipitous fall in the value of your 25 shares, yet kept your faith in the company. You put in an order to buy 1000 shares at 50 cents because your purchases are always in $500 groups (see previous chapter). You now have 1025 shares at an average purchase price of just under $1 each. In three years they appreciate ten times and look to go even higher in years to come! Not bad for a little deeper thinking on your part, eh?

Another personal example is the case of the Dana corporation. They had just been kicked out of the S&P 500 after becoming a victim of the US motor vehicle downturn in 2004, and I could see the tremendous rise in the number of shares being sold every day and the drastic lowering of the price. Like with Ericsson, by using conse- quential thinking I could see that the selling pressures were not a function of Dana's fundamental value so I felt confident the company would survive. I put in an order to buy 2000 at $1.08, another order for 10,000 at 88 cents, and another order for 15,000 at 77 cents, all of which I got, although I did not get my last order which was for 50,000 at 27 cents. This all happened within a two-day period, right at the end of the previous weeks of heavy selling. I came away with 36,000 shares in Dana Corporation. The shares then rebounded towards the $2 range, and so on the basis of "a man who takes his profit never loses" I sold 25,000 of them and more than doubled the money I had spent. No doubt I would have done better to keep them for the long term, but collecting a nice seven day doubling of profit was very tempting, and I have no regrets.

Such dramatic fluctuations happen to individual stocks occasionally. Given the stock market as a whole, such fluctuations happen perhaps twice a year. If you want to catch these buying opportunities, you will have to keep an eye on the market from time to time. Such occurrences are generally broadcast by the media. The main thing to know is that when a substantial company with a fundamentally good stock is out of favor, it is generally a good time to buy.

CHAPTER EIGHT

Commodities: the truth behind the market

In investing circles, trading in commodities is like trading in stocks. You can buy and sell commodities just like shares. Commodities are defined as a certain quantity of desirable items (usually the product of agriculture or mining) that somebody at some time wants delivered to their doorstep. For example, farmers grow wheat, corn, and alfalfa, and need to see their product sold. Large farmers, or farmers' cooperatives, sell on the "Commodities Exchange" based in Chicago. Often they are contacted by brokers who inquire if the farmer wishes to sell through them; likewise with oil and coal. At the Commodities Exchange, investors can also buy and sell these products, speculating that the price will go up or down. The investors do not want the product actually delivered and plan to sell before that time, so they buy contracts known as "Futures" because the contract will be fulfilled and the product actually sold sometime in the future. They are betting that the price will go up if they are buying or betting that the price will go down if they are selling "short".

It is true that there is a lot of quick money to be made in commodities. But it is equally true that there are a lot of quick losses. In fact, a large loss is the usual outcome for about 90% of the non-professional investors who trade in the commodity market. Commodity trading is like weather forecasting; how frequently have we found that when we get to a place where we have been told will have good weather, the weather is not as indicated? Such is the way with commodities.

Commodities are presently sold in four main segments:

1. Metal and Petroleum Futures: These include gold, silver, copper and platinum which are sold by the troy ounce or pound, and petroleum which is usually sold by the barrel, pound, BTU or gallon.

2. Agricultural Futures: These include wheat, corn, cotton, soybeans and the like which are usually sold by the bushel, pound, gallon, cents or hundredweight.

3. Currency Futures: These include all of the "tradable currencies" of the world (all those currencies that are interchangeable with each other) but exclude ones which have high inflation rates or are pegged to another currency. Examples: the U.S. dollar, the E.U. euro, British pound, Swiss frank, Mexican peso, Japanese yen, Australian dollar, and Singapore or Hong Kong dollars. Currencies are usually traded in many thousands of the various money denominations.

4. Index Futures: These include the DJ (Dow Jones) industrial average, the Mini DJ industrial average, the S&P Index, the Mini S&P 500, the NASDAQ 100, the Mini NASDAQ, the Russell 1000, and the US Dollar Index.

There are other futures available. These come and go since brokers and professional speculators are always coming out with new futures, and countries have many different commodities which they sell. The commodities market is very complex, and even the experts are not able to grasp it all.

The maintenance (holding) deposit

In the commodities market, you buy, not the commodities themselves, but an option to buy in the future. Your investment generally equals about 5% of the commodity's total value. This is called a maintenance or holding deposit. If you want to actually own the commodity, you will have to pay its whole value. But the stock exchange knows you're playing the market—they know you don't intend to take delivery—and so the exchange protects itself by insisting they hold a specific amount of your money in deposit, generally 5% or higher, to cover any possible losses in your position. When buying a commodity, therefore, your costs include the usual commission costs of buying (or selling) combined with the holding deposit.

For instance, if you have an option to buy $40,000 worth of soybeans, your contract may cost only $1,000 (or 2.2%), which fee is held by the broker until the position is liquidated, at which point you get the deposit back along with any profit. This sounds reasonable until the position goes against you—in other words, the price goes down. The same amount of soybeans may be selling for $35,000, say. You have to come up with the difference, or $5,000, for your broker. He will give you a maintenance call, telling you that the holding fee has increased. You must wire your broker or account executive more money in order to maintain the ownership of your position. The reason you would have to wire in additional funds is because commodity markets require sufficient deposits at all times to cover any possible deficits the exchange might incur when it has to pay the farmer or producer the amount of the contract. If you do not wire the needed funds immediately, they have the right to sell you out and demand payment of the balance. They will come after you to repay them, whether by court or some other means. Then you really will not sleep at night. I know because it has happened to me.

There always has to be a surplus in your deposit or the brokers will sell the position to limit their losses. Even with the system of deposits, commodities brokers still sometimes have to pay out of their own pocket if their clients are unable to do so. The brokers are liable to the exchange also.

The minimum amount of money that you have to pay in order to keep your account varies for each commodity. The greater the volatility of the commodity (i.e. the price's up and down movement), the higher the required standby deposit to hold it. The amount of the deposit is set by the exchange for that particular contract. The exchange will always increase the holding price of a contract if there is a lot of speculation in it because it means that there is a higher risk of an investor's defaulting. When this happens, you suddenly have to pay more even if you already own the contract. You will have to add to your deposit, and that extra amount is the difference between what you've already paid and what the new holding price is, as determined by the exchange. Thus the exchange can dampen the enthusiasm of those who have by their actions sent the commodity's price up or down beyond the normal trading activity.

In addition to market fluctuations, there are any number of unforeseen events that could cause your position to go against you. Casual investors seem to think that commodities will go higher, and over the years they do but not before there is some downward pressure from time to time. The problem is that to hold any position in a commodity for a long period, such as years, means that the maintenance (holding) costs would be so great as to nullify any eventual profit. Notwithstanding maintenance calls, there is a maintenance fee every three to six months of around 10% of your original investment. If you had bought an option for $6,000, you might have to pay $300 every six to nine months. The commodity market thus discourages long-term investment.

My foray into commodities

I have dabbled in commodities on several occasions but not in the past twenty-five years. There was a time when commodities appeared very attractive to me. Stocks were a slow means of earning money, but commodities seemed quick. Why, in one day, it was possible to make several thousand dollars if you were right in your price assessment.

My first foray into commodities was a lucky accident . An account executive with a silver-options company called me out of the blue to introduce me to trading in silver. He suggested that there was a good chance of making money by buying an option to purchase a 10,000 ounce silver contract. "Why," he said, "your silver contract has only to go up about ten cents per ounce and you will have paid for the option costs and would then be in a position to make a lot of money!" The option cost was $6,000 and it just so happened that I had the money spare at the time. So I purchased a year's contract and ended up getting hooked like a fish on the value of commodities; I bought and sold various different types over the next three years, including grains, the British pound, sugar, pork bellies, beef, copper and gold.

Why did I get so hooked? Because I made a profit of $50,000 on my first purchase of the 10,000 ounces of silver! My silver option coincided with the Hunt brothers' attempts to corner the silver market in the late 1970s. They were wealthy and were able to control the price for a time by buying millions of dollars' worth of silver options. This made the price go up. It was pure luck on my part that I purchased the option about five months before this cornering, which caused a sharp upturn in the silver market. I had disturbed sleep for several months while I saw the price go up day after day. Why was I nervous about a price that was going in my favor? Because what goes up must come down! Had I waited until my option expired in another three weeks I could have more than doubled my profit, but I was happy for my health's sake to get out a bit early with a nice profit of $50,000.

The whole affair was actually one of those things that happen perhaps once in a lifetime. The prices of commodities don't usually change dramatically in a year's time, but I didn't know that; I was naïve. It was, after all, my first try. The fact that it proved successful was pure luck and required no skill, but I did not appreciate this at the time. I thought I knew what I was doing. As I said, I was hooked.

One time I purchased two contracts of wheat at a certain price which I thought was attractive in view of the various weather predictions for the grain-growing countries. The information predicting shortages was found in the various business sections of newspapers. Unfortunately the price did not go up within the week as predicted but instead started to go down. It was then reported in the media that there had been a forecast of unexpected rain that would relieve the drought. So I sold my two contracts for a loss, as it was indicated that there would now be plenty of grain world-wide. After I had sold the two contracts, the price of grains started to move up again. I was being what's called "whip-sawed"—buying or selling just before the price went against me either up or down. My account executive seemed to think that I was just unlucky, and if I persevered all would be well. He also no doubt enjoyed the various commissions he received from my activity. The truth is, the clue to my success or failure was staring me in the face, but I did not discover it until later.

Next, I decided to try the long term and so I bought two contracts that were six and nine months away, allowing me to take advantage of the steady rise in price over time. I also decided that if I doubled up on the contracts at several different prices, my average cost per contract would be lower; that is, if I purchased a contract for wheat at $2.80 per bushel and then purchased another contract at $3.20 per bushel, then my average for the two contracts would be $3.00. Did I make some money? Yes I made some, and I lost some, too! And the tendency to lose was greater than the tendency to win.

While I was in England on one occasion, I saw the headlines that the coal miners were going to go on strike. It seemed to me that the British pound would go down in value very shortly because people don't want to invest in England when major strikes are taking place. So I called my account executive in the United States and told him to sell four contracts of British pounds immediately. Within a week I had made about $20,000 because, to begin with, my initial sell had managed to catch the beginning of the first of several violent swings in the price of the pound. Next, I was able to buy and sell at the lows and highs of the prices for three consecutive swings. Basically, I sold near the high, the pound dropped, then I reversed my position until it went back up a few points, then I reversed again.

I was feeling as if I had the commodities market licked and that I knew what I was doing. However, I was wrong. Slowly but surely each of the commodities that I dabbled in lost money—not a lot, because I was very circumspect about what I did and I read up on a particular commodity exhaustively before I made my play—but somehow, notwithstanding all of my research, I did not have the success needed to stay in the game. Instead, I was losing money on a consistent basis. You will notice that I use the word *play* and *game*. That is because that is what it was.

On two occasions I delved too deeply into the market and bought too many contracts. The resulting financial loss was very embarrassing. I finally had to sit back and examine all of my plays and try to work out what I was doing wrong. First, I discovered that if I had traded the exact opposite to what I had done I would have come out with a nice profit instead of a bad loss. Yet how was I to work out a strategy that always took the opposite of what seemed to be the best course of action? A very difficult exercise to do, honestly. I knew of people who had made a lot of money in commodities, famous traders. I also knew that people who worked at the commodities exchange regularly made substantial profits. Yet I also knew that these people couldn't take the pressure of trading much beyond the age of thirty-five to forty years of age or for very long. I had to ask myself why that might be. Then it hit me: the people who made the big money were the people on the floor of the stock exchange. Why was this? *Because they were there!*

It became clear to me that anyone wishing to make money in the commodity market had to *be at the market*, not at the end of a phone being advised by an account executive who heard of some event several hours or more *after* those on the exchange floor, and the executive could only advise his customers later than that. There was one clue that had been staring me in the face: the papers, the TV, the magazines were all giving news that was at least one day old, if not several days old. In commodities, I realized, you don't want day-old news—you need up-to-the-second news. And so I came to realize that the ordinary man in the street, trying to guess the possible movement of the market, did not have a hope of succeeding in the long term because of his old news. He has to gamble blindly, as I had done for three years. I hated to be beaten. The market could become very addictive—but it is also very destructive.

Floor professionals are in the best position to routinely sell or buy commodities on a daily basis because they are immediately informed if there is a major event or even a rumor of one, both which affect the prices. Because these people are on the floor, they are the first to be able to take advantage of that information and buy or sell accordingly. There is a saying I had heard a number of times: "Professionals buy on the rumor and sell on the fact." That is how floor professionals trade each day. They do not hold positions overnight. Something might happen overnight that would cause them to be sandwiched. For a professional trader to hold commodity positions over a weekend or a holiday is almost unheard of.

The interesting thing is, these floor traders' actions start a directional movement in the commodity and even in related commodities. When the news filters to the brokers and agents (after the floor traders have made their moves), they in turn participate in the buying and selling and further accelerate the movement. Then come the speculators who are closely in touch with the market and finally the more remote investors, such as the hobby traders, who are the last to participate. The floor traders and commodity brokers, having learned that in general it is best to be out of the market by the end of the day, get out, take their profits, and go home to a restful night's sleep. The casual investor, having received the "hot" news in the paper, finally decides to participate, only to find that at the end of the day prices have settled lower due to profit taking (or selling) by the profess-sionals. The price is too low to sell now, so the casual investor—you— is forced to keep their position overnight and wire in additional funds if they have a maintenance call. So the man on the street—that is, you or I—is in a very bad position.

Rumors in the commodities exchange spread like wildfire. The professionals do not much care whether the rumor is fact or fiction. They will act on the news first and get out as soon as there's a profit. They're not interested in holding a position for long. They know that most often there is a reversal of prices, either up or down, during the same day and that consequently the greatest money is to be made in the short term. Unfortunately, the man on the street cannot act as quickly. By the time such rumors have come to public knowledge, what was "true" yesterday is untrue today, even though it is reported in the news as "true". This is *the* reason why making trading decisions based on "hot" news in the media is not a good idea. You are oper-ating on old information.

Back to my story, I finally realized what I was up against: the rumors which indicate something might happen that then does not. I finally grasped that I could never win on a permanent basis unless I were to spend my time close to the market floor in Chicago, trading every day, never long term. Not only that, but any money I made would incur a short-term capital gains tax! If I were to go that route, what would happen to all of my other work, to my family, or my commitments to others? I saw it all! The only way I could come out winning was at the expense of everything else I did. I did not want such a drastic change in my life. So I backed away from trading in commodities after having been slowly crucified for several years. I did a 180-degree turn, got out and have never been back.

Interesting facts about "stop losses"

Commodity brokers and account executives will tell you that you can prevent losing too much money on the exchange by using stop-losses. You can limit your loss on any commodity by placing a "stop loss" in your buy-or-sell order, which is a point above or below the price where your contract will definitely be sold. For example, if I had purchased some wool contracts and was "long" (that is, expected the price of wool to increase) then it would be recommended that I place a stop loss below my buying price which would make sure that there would be a limit to how much I could lose if the price went down—at least, this is the way it's supposed to work. In actual fact, a stop loss guarantees nothing. This is because placing a stop loss at a given price in no way guarantees that it will be sold at that price. In practice, it is often sold at a worse price. This is because there may be *nobody* willing to purchase your contract at your stop-loss price, in which case it will have to be sold at the next available bid price—the one at which other traders will buy, if there is such a person on that day's market session.

The problem is, every market player knows that the exchange sets a "limit move" on commodities. Each one is regulated to go down (or up) by only a certain amount in any one day. Buyers do not want to buy too soon, and because of this, sellers cannot sell. This has happened many times in the past. For example, there was the Mad Cow scare; the cattle-related commodities went the allowable limit down for several days—each time so fast (near instantaneously) that those who wanted to sell could not do it; nobody wanted to buy their positions because the buyers knew the contracts were going to go down further. This caused great financial stress to many who had "long" positions and who saw their positions getting worse and worse without being able to get out, despite the fact that they had "stop losses."

How might this work more specifically? Let me give you an example: If I were to buy a February Cattle contract for 91 cents per pound and each contract was for 40,000 pounds, then I might be encouraged to put in a stop-loss order at 88 cents per pound so that the maximum that I could lose would be three cents per pound, or a loss of $1,200. But then let us say that, due to certain bad news, the cattle prices went down at the opening of the market instantaneously by their daily allowed limit of ten cents, and no one was willing to buy my contract at 88 cents. I would stand to lose heavily because that limit down would mean that I would already have a loss of $4,000 (ten cents times 40,000) despite the fact that I had a stop loss that was supposed to limit my loss to $1,200! And the question now becomes, how much more will it go down tomorrow or the next day, if there are more limit-down moves? You might say that this could never happen or is very unlikely, but do you really want to have a chance of being on the wrong side? What if there was a sudden report of a civil war in a coffee-producing nation? Such things have happened in the past. Earthquakes, strikes by workers, major storms or such can and do happen, always when least expected. Knowing all this, the question might now be asked, "How can I really and surely limit my loss?" The short answer is, in the commodities market, you cannot!

Now, in addition to stop-loss orders being incapable of guaranteeing a limit to your losses, there is yet another factor to them. I remember while I was investing in commodities, it seemed strange to me that from time to time various commodities had extreme gyrations up and down in a given day. I was interested in wool contracts. On one day I saw the contract start out at a given price, drop steadily all morning until just after lunch, after which it retraced upwards to its original opening price. Why is this happening, I asked myself?

The answer to this question lies in the recommendations of commodity traders for their clients to have stop-loss orders. These orders cause your commodity to become liable to being what is called "raided" by one or more people. In this raiding, it is possible for somebody with a lot of money to sell or buy in order to push the price of a commodity to the extreme. By suddenly selling, he can lower the price (or by buying, increase the price) thereby triggering some of the stop losses which then accentuate the price's movement in the direction wanted. At some point, this person with deep pockets totally reverses his position, meaning he goes long if he was short (or starts buying if he was selling) and makes a handsome profit from the maneuver. Although it is illegal for a group of people to get together to do this, it still happens.

The floor traders also love stop losses because they know the extent of such orders. They know that if they can breach a certain resistance level in a commodity, the subsequent majority of "stops" will become self-feeding to carry the commodity in a continuing direction. Having the commodity carried in a direction by progressive stop losses enables traders on the floor to buy into a down swing, or, conversely, to sell into an upswing, pick the right place to reverse their positions, and then get out at a higher or lower price for a nice day's profit!

Limit moves are the biggest danger to your entry into the commodities market. As explained, a "limit move" is the maximum amount of movement a price can make in one day and is something that the exchange controls in order to limit the market's daily swings, especially under exceptional happenings. This limit in movement prevents sudden extreme fluctuations that might be caused by some unexpected news like an assassination. Limit moves happen on a fairly regular basis but usually in only one or another of the commodities that are traded. If you are on the wrong side, there will essentially be no sellers (if it is moving limit up) or buyers (if it is moving limit down). In other words, you might urgently wish to sell your position, yet be unable to because no one wishes to stand in front of a steamroller. Why expect anyone to purchase your position when it might make another limit down move the next day and keep going? If this happens to you, your contract will be automatically sold by your broker and you will take a huge loss for which you will be completely liable! It is small comfort to know that commodity traders are generally somewhat lenient towards their debtors and will work with you to help you pay it off over time.

I was sold out about three times. The price went down so far that my holding fee was insufficient. The brokers wanted more money. I'd like to tell you that this amount was based on some fixed formula, but the formula changes according to somewhat arbitrary decisions by the commodity exchange, based on their perception of the market volatility. This happened to the aforementioned Hunt brothers who were trying to corner the silver market. The holding costs for their silver contracts increased because of the high speculative activity in silver, and they suffered huge losses because they were not able to pay the increased costs.

One time I thought my broker had jumped the gun, as it were, and that he should have waited a little longer. I felt that I had been treated unfairly. At the time I was particularly short of ready funds, having placed all my spare money into the commodity account. I could have borrowed some money on my credit card but didn't want to dig the hole any deeper. The brokerage firm had done a lot of business with me, and I felt that there were extenuating circumstances in the amount they were claiming I owed.

The following day I had a call from one of the managers of the brokerage company. He said the position was serious and asked how much I could pay. I said that I was prepared to pay a certain amount, borrowing from my business line of credit, but that it wasn't really proper for me to do this and that such an amount would have to completely clear the outstanding balance.

"Fine," he said. "How soon can you send it?"

"Later today," I said. The amount that I sent was equivalent to about one quarter of the amount they wanted. I sent off the check with a notation written in the bottom left hand corner that said, "In full and final settlement of all account claims." I noted afterwards that my check had been cashed.

About five weeks later I had a phone call from a debt collector who demanded the balance of the money. I said that I had sent a check in full settlement and would be pleased to fax them a copy of it. There was silence on the other end of the phone. Finally the debt collector said that it was highly unusual, but could I send them a copy of both sides of the cancelled check? This I did and never heard another word from them. This experience, in addition to my new understanding of the need to be on the floor in order to get ahead, was the end of my foray into the commodities market.

The good use of commodities

The commodities market is an advantage to those persons and companies who have something to sell, plus those who genuinely want to buy those commodities. This is where supply and demand come into play. A farmer who is getting ready to harvest a crop can keep an eye on the commodity market, and if it is seen that the crop can be sold at a good profit, he might consider locking in a profitable price by selling the appropriate number of contracts. The cattle or pig farmer can do the same. They will be able to get that price even if the market price later goes lower; of course, they will not get any increase in price if the market goes higher. However, for the farmer there is no risk involved—he has locked in a price that will give him a good profit. Likewise, metal producers, say of copper or tin, can also lock in a price they like and sell well into the future; similarly, users of precious metals such as gold can buy and lock in prices that are acceptable to them. In these cases, whether the commodities go up or down essentially makes no difference to them. They have factored in the prices they are comfortable with and because they are either a producer or buyer, there is no underlying risk. Rather, the commodities market acts for them like a hedge against future risk.

The true function of the commodities market is to facilitate the smooth and orderly transition from the producer to the buyer at prices that allow for supply and demand. If there is too much of a commodity available, the price automatically falls. Likewise, if demand for a commodity exceeds the supply, then the price moves up until there is a balance between the wants and needs of both the seller and buyer. This supply and demand rules the world in a multi-faceted pattern and although sometimes efforts are made by governments to prevent it, it is a principle which marches on and cannot truly be stopped. So, in fine, there are good reasons to have commodities markets, but all of this gambling on the gyrations is just that— gambling. If you want a little gamble then take it, but you will have more fun going to Las Vegas or on a cruise.

Conclusion

I have come to the conclusion in my own life that commodities have no place in a prudent long-term investor's plans. The daily time needed to pursue the investment is disproportionate to the final outcome, leaving little time for those other pursuits that one might normally have. In addition, it can have a negative effect on one's mental and physical health. With the very best information, your plans will go wrong. Unexpected statistics that are reported by outsiders will suddenly reverse a commodity's direction. Over-seas wars, famine, sudden rain or lack of it in places such as India, Australia, China, or Russia will gyrate commodities in ways that lead the investor to often lose heavily. The casual (or even active) commodities investor working from home has the odds stacked against them as they are behind the curve instead of in front of it.

The truth is, as a man on the street, investing in commodity markets without having or wanting the product is gambling. Unfortunately, gambling in commodities can and often will take you for much more than you can afford! Make no mistake about it, you are much more likely to lose long term than gain. Unless you operate often on the actual floor of the commodities exchange, you have very little chance of success as a short-term trader. Investing in commodities is always against the ordinary man on the street who thinks to make some money through it. The commodities investor has only the gambler's rewards of excitement when things go well and frustration when they

223

do not, with little guarantee of winning. Rather, the place to invest is in the stock market or property; both are solid investment vehicles and excellent places to invest your money.

About the Author

Gordon Griffin was born just outside London, England in 1930. During the Depression, the family had little to give their five children so, at age seven, Gordon started going door to door selling broken orange crates for firewood. During World War II, he was evacuated to Wales (1939-1943) and placed with various foster families. There he sold his coat in order to raise the money to return home.

Government School in those days terminated at age 12. By age 13, Gordon, like other boys his age, went to work. His first job was as an office boy for Cable and Wireless. After hours, he made earrings and bracelets that he sold to the secretaries. He knew that he wanted to have his own business, but he also knew that, to have a real business, he had to have some money as capital.

In 1947, Gordon enlisted in the British Army for four years, planning, during that time, to save up a "tidy bit." At the same time, he was wondering what sort of business to have. Should he rent boats on the Thames? Sell Tiger Balm ointment? During a three-month leave in 1953, while helping a farmer with the hay, he found a large edible mushroom in the field. He picked it and gave it to the farmer's wife, who was delighted to receive it. She told Gordon there was a man nearby who grew mushrooms for a living. Would he like to meet him?

The long and short of it was, that he ending up building a mushroom farm. Five years later, he and his wife had the opportunity to sell their farm and emigrate to Tasmania, Australia, where they started their farm anew. Some 12 years later, he had the opportunity to emigrate to the United States and build a mushroom farm in Fillmore, Utah, that is still operational today.

Along the way, Gordon invented a composting machine for the Mushroom Industry, and patented twenty or so other inventions. He has written a book about inventing, called T*he Survivor Manual for Inventors*, published by John Wiley in 1991.

He purchased land in both Tasmania and Utah, starting his own land development company, called Devon Dee Inc. Finally he partnered with others in acquiring mining rights to a volcano in Fillmore Utah. "Do you know anyone who owns a volcano?" he likes to ask. Lava rock from the mine is sold for various purposes (see www.RedDome.com).

Gordon calls this book "a labor of love." He has a passion for helping others become financially successful. He says, "I wish you all success!"

www.ingramcontent.com/pod-product-compliance
Lightning Source LLC
Chambersburg PA
CBHW080803180526
45168CB00006B/2316